RETHINK PROPERTY INVESTING

BECOME FINANCIALLY FREE WITH
COMMERCIAL PROPERTY INVESTING

RETHINK PROPERTY INVESTING

SCOTT O'NEILL
MINA O'NEILL

WILEY

First published in 2021 by John Wiley & Sons Australia, Ltd
42 McDougall St, Milton Qld 4064
Office also in Melbourne

Typeset in Liberation Serif 11pt/14pt

ISBN: 978-0-730-39152-4

A catalogue record for this
book is available from the
National Library of Australia

NATIONAL
LIBRARY
OF AUSTRALIA

Cover design by Wiley

Front cover image: © bingokid / Getty Images

Back cover photo: © Melinda Hird

Table sources: **Tables 1 and 2:** The Australian Taxation Office Taxation, Statistics 2017-18, Individuals - Table 27, Sourced on 15 December 2020, <https://data.gov.au/data/dataset/taxation-statistics-2017-18>. **Table 4:** 1990 data: Peter Abelson and Demi Chung. The Real Story of Housing Prices in Australia from 1970 to 2003.The Australian Economic Review. 2005, Vol 38, Issues 3, pp. 265-281. <https://doi.org/10.1111/j.1467-8462.2005.00373>. 2020 data: Australian Bureau of Statistics 2020 'Tables 4 and 5. Median price unstratified and number of transfers capital city and rest of state, Residential Property Price Indexes: Eight Capital Cities, <https://www.abs.gov.au/statistics/economy/price-indexes-and-inflation/residential-property-price-indexes-eight-capital-cities/latest-release>, accessed 12 January 2021. **Table 7:** Australian Bureau of Statistics 2020 'Tables 4 and 5. Median price unstratified and number of transfers capital city and rest of state, Residential Property Price Indexes: Eight Capital Cities, <https://www.abs.gov.au/statistics/economy/price-indexes-and-inflation/residential-property-price-indexes-eight-capital-cities/latest-release>, accessed 12 January 2021.

Disclaimer
The material in this publication is of the nature of general comment only, and does not represent professional advice. It is not intended to provide specific guidance for particular circumstances and it should not be relied on as the basis for any decision to take action or not take action on any matter which it covers. Readers should obtain professional advice where appropriate, before making any such decision. To the maximum extent permitted by law, the authors and publisher disclaim all responsibility and liability to any person, arising directly or indirectly from any person taking or not taking action based on the information in this publication.

CONTENTS

PREFACE

31 degrees. Sun on my face. Sand between my toes. Life was pretty relaxed as we lay on a beach on Kos, in the Greek islands. It was 2016 and Mina and I were relishing a six-month break from Australia.

We thought we'd hit the jackpot. I had retired from my day job at age 28. At that time we owned 25 residential and commercial properties scattered across four different states. It hadn't come easily or by accident, though; we'd worked hard, saved for many years and obsessed over every property decision we made. Thousands of hours had gone into building this portfolio. But we had won back time in our pursuit of a lifelong ambition—to replace both of our incomes so in future we could do what we wanted on our own terms.

Now we had taken the brakes off and flown to Greece to eat, drink, visit family and travel around Europe for six whole months, using the passive income we had earned from our properties. It was a deeply humbling feeling.

As I sat by the water and watched the beach chairs being stacked away for winter (signalling it was nearly time to go home), I mentally reviewed our expenses over the past few months. After all our accommodation, plane tickets, eating out and other expenses were added up, our properties still produced more income than we spent. This was our 'aha' moment, when we knew life would be different forever. I couldn't believe it!

Our property income was now enough for us to live off—and retire on. It was one of the most exciting moments I have ever felt, because I knew we had 'made it' financially. And there was no reason why we couldn't keep travelling indefinitely. I felt like we had none of the stresses normally triggered by having to go back to jobs neither of us enjoyed.

However, there was an empty feeling there too, like something was missing, which was strange considering we had reached such a long-held personal goal. It made me think, what's next? How had we got here? We had been offering some investing advice on the side; maybe we could take this to the next level and use our experience as a platform to teach others? And why not? We seemed to be the only people I knew at the time chasing this high-yielding commercial and residential investing strategy that worked so well for us. Many others in the industry were preaching outdated and slower ways to build wealth that we simply didn't agree with. We could see there was an opportunity to show people what to do and how to do it, and just what was achievable.

It struck me then that our success owed much to the fact that we have always looked beyond our own backyard. Beyond our familiar territory in Sydney, and even beyond the traditional investment focus of residential property—to commercial property. We like to do things differently, to challenge the status quo. We like to take calculated risks, and we soon realised that you *can* invest outside of where you live. You *can* look to different asset classes to get you there, and discover that the local residential market is *not* the only way.

Our success has come from our move to invest in the commercial property market. It has held the key to our future wealth and underpinned why we set up our business, Rethink Investing, to help others on the same road. More than 2000 investors and counting, in fact.

As a result, we're part of a new generation of investors. We invest very differently from our parents, finding a different path from the one they followed to create their wealth. We chose to focus on higher cash flow investments rather than the outdated negative gearing model, because it works.

Four years after that 'aha' moment on the beach, life is very different. When we sat down to write this book, the world had been hit by the coronavirus pandemic. With a newborn baby in our family and like everyone else, we hunkered down, practised 'social distancing' and joined the effort to try to 'flatten the curve', two novel concepts that have become intimately familiar to all of us this past year. To our surprise only one of our nine commercial property incomes has been impacted by COVID-19.

In the very early days the pandemic affected everything in our business. Things slowed right down in March and April 2020, but they picked up again in May, June and July, after which we experienced some of our busiest months ever. We attribute this rebound to a few factors. Facing job uncertainty, people are more than ever looking for high cash flow. Secondly, the record low interest rates are giving people more reason to invest their cash. Finally, many people now have extra time to concentrate on their investing rather than travelling or working non-stop.

We believe that investing now is one of the greatest opportunities we will ever see. With our commercial properties, we're seeing net yields of 7 per cent plus, with interest rates under 3 per cent. That's a 4 per cent gap! Historically, we expect to see a gap of 2 per cent. This means right now there's the opportunity of a lifetime to get the best cash flow returns ever in commercial property. This, in turn, should result in strong capital growth as the gap between these two metrics narrows.

Our message is simple. Don't think of commercial property as a risky investment just because we're in a pandemic. We target the most resilient types of businesses. As we've seen, our strategy of buying medical, logistics, and other essential services–type investments with strong tenants has proven to be very resilient. In the residential property sector we always target properties that are relatively affordable for both tenants and home buyers while still being in good growth areas with strong yields. And tight vacancy rates are also a must.

I want to use these pages to explain to you how some commercial and residential properties will perform very differently in the COVID-19 environment.

First, how has the coronavirus affected the commercial market? The answer is that the effect has varied greatly. For example, CBD office space has struggled, and will continue to do so. Fewer people will commute to our capital city centres on public transport in order to sit in an airconditioned office tower where the risk of infection is greater.

Retail is another property type facing harder times. Forced closures have made it difficult for customers to visit their favourite stores, which has led to more online purchasing. This leads me to the opportunity part. As more people purchase goods online, there is a greater need for logistics and storage. This has meant that warehouses in many areas have been more in demand from tenants and owners alike.

Medical properties and other essential service–type businesses have also powered through the COVID-19 environment with greater ease, compared with the discretionary spending, retail-type businesses.

There are many reasons why each type of business will perform better or worse in this climate, but we've always said that property is a long game. So you need to see the bigger picture and understand how businesses work in general before you buy property. In relation to COVID-19, here's what we're seeing:

- *Interest rates.* These are at all-time lows and they don't look like they will rise for a long time. This means the net cash flow you receive on your commercial property has never been better.

- *Due diligence.* This has never been easier to complete. Before COVID-19, it was much harder to distinguish a strong business from a weak one. This is because a key marker when assessing a property purchase—how a tenant will perform—is easier to determine during the pandemic. We ask for bank statements, because from them we can readily check if the tenant has paid 100 per cent of their rent, if they've had no rental reduction and no JobKeeper allowances, and if they have retained the same number of employees through the tough times. This gives us a lot of confidence in the business prior to purchase.

- *Growth.* Commercial property is growing in value off the back of falling interest rates and increased buyer demand. There is also a severe shortage of stock. In some areas stock levels have fallen by 50 per cent, with many owners reluctant to sell their assets while they see no better options out there for making a good return on their investment. Increased demand but lower supply is fuelling the growth equation. Of course, some sectors are suffering (such as the CBD office market, as noted), but others have never seen *such* great demand. This demand is largely from residential investors who have turned to commercial property in search of better returns. Increased demand over limited supply = capital growth, which is the central premise of the book you are now holding.

All of the knowledge and experience we have built up over the years informs the way we help our clients through our business, Rethink Investing, and in turn inspired us to write this book, in which we offer guidance to help you on your own journey to wealth and independence.

There's much to learn, but we were determined to keep it engaging and relatable, drawing on our '7 Steps', a blueprint we use every day when working with our clients.

We'll share our own story too, so you can better understand our passion for commercial property investing. Our long-held passion is to help others on their investing journey and to reach out to more and more people by sharing a proven process that can be replicated again and again.

As we have grown, so has our portfolio—now valued at well over $20 million. At the time of writing we enjoy a passive income (after our home mortgage has been taken care of) of more than $450000 a year from 32 properties. With the exception of 2020 (constrained by COVID-19 travel restrictions), we still travel to Europe every year to visit family and escape Australia's winter for Greece's summer. After 'rentvesting' for nearly 10 years, we finally bought a family home to live in. Later we will explain why we decided to set up our investment portfolio before we purchased a principal place of residence (PPOR).

Back at the start of our journey, the option of investing in commercial property seemed like it was out of our reach, but now we embrace it, confident in its power as a tool for building passive wealth. We made it happen by taking risks and pivoting from the typical.

As you read this book you'll find that, with a few exceptions, we speak to you with one voice. We've always invested in property together, and have shared the load in running our business, so rather than attributing every decision or action to one or the other of us, it made sense to simplify matters by using the first-person plural.

Of course we bring different strengths to the business. Mina looks after the property management and running our portfolio. This includes managing the many insurances, tax matters, different rental managers and the general day to day of the portfolio. With 32 properties this is a big job that needs extremely good organisational skills, one of Mina's strengths. She also basically built the business, including all backend, databases, business structure, marketing, website design management, administration, accounting, HR—you name it!

Scott's greatest skills include understanding the market and negotiating purchases while following first principles—in a nutshell, buying the right property in the right market at the right price. He has negotiated thousands of property purchases for Rethink Investing's clients. This depth of experience is one of the reasons we have done so well.

See you on the other side of the backyard fence!

INTRODUCTION

Scott's story

Creating a $20 million plus property portfolio doesn't happen overnight. It doesn't happen in your own backyard either. The path I took was shaped by a childhood and early adulthood spent obsessing over the Australian property market.

I learned the foundations of property investing a lot earlier than most, as a youngster growing up in Sydney, through patience, persistence and playing the market. I grew up in the Sutherland Shire with two younger sisters. My parents worked hard, Dad as an accountant and Mum as an engineer draughtsperson. They were also keen property investors. I learned a lot from them as investors, even though they followed a very different strategy from the one I ended up adopting.

Their strategy, which was a common one in the eighties, nineties and noughties, was to buy negatively geared properties and collect a larger than normal tax return in return for a cash flow loss on property. What bothered me about this strategy was that generally it was effective only if you had a large PAYG taxable income that could be offset by a loss through property income. This meant you needed to show a cash flow loss from your properties just so you could get some extra tax back in your tax return. To me this didn't seem like an avenue to retirement. How can you achieve your retirement goals if your properties don't provide positive cash flow? The answer is you can't, so it wasn't an approach I wanted to replicate, especially since house prices were getting so high compared with my income.

Rather than acquiring a property to generate a cash flow loss in the name of a tax refund, I wanted to buy properties that made month-to-month cash flow–based profits, as any good business should. I viewed building an investment portfolio as just like building a business. I don't know any business that goes out there to deliberately make a cash flow loss just to claw some extra tax back later.

Don't get me wrong. I do recognise the long-term benefits of capital growth with the negatively geared tax outcome on property investing. It's just that I want the instant profit that higher cash flow assets can offer. What I have found throughout my investment career is that some of my highest yielding investments have also produced some of the highest growth rates. So I don't buy into the idea that you have to choose either cash flow or growth. The truth is you probably want both. This realisation helped shift my investment mindset towards a positively geared one.

To better explain how I view property investing, I use the simple analogy of a café business. The way I see it, you wouldn't go and buy a café to lose $100 000 cash flow on the understanding that you'd be able to claim $30 000 back. I would prefer to make $100 000 cash flow and then pay 30 per cent tax. I have always thought that making money is better than saving tax. It's remarkable how many people get this part of property investing wrong. Getting on the right side of this simple cash flow equation was a vital part of my early investing journey.

At the age of 17, I already knew I wanted to get into the market. So I got together with a close mate and we pooled our modest savings from regular part-time and casual gigs: at McDonald's, cleaning cars at dealerships and working as a surveyor field hand. Off we trotted to the bank with our hard-earned savings (which represented about a 5 per cent deposit on a unit we were looking at). As you would imagine, the bank said no deal and to come back when we had more savings and full-time jobs. We felt rejected, but not deterred.

After I finished school I started studying for an engineering degree at Sydney University. While studying I managed to secure an average of four shifts a week at the Sharks Leagues club and during the university summer breaks I took extended working holidays. One highlight was spending a ski season in Whistler, Canada, when I was 20. I worked as a cook in the Longhorn Saloon, which helped fund the trip, and even got to have an amazing heli-skiing adventure in the Rocky Mountains. A year later I moved to the Gold Coast for the surfing. I worked in a famous Gold Coast nightclub into the early hours of the morning and was clocking up some good travelling experiences too.

Possibly without realising it, I was laying the foundations for my future career in property. Working hard to earn money while studying was important, because it meant that instead of being flat broke I was thinking about buying a property.

These early experiences of working outside of my hometown helped break down a lot of mental barriers when it came to investing. To me, all of Australia was my backyard. My growing familiarity with other areas meant I was not bound to certain locations. This mindset was extremely important in the grand scheme of things. It would later even help me purchase a property overseas.

After travelling and working, I somehow finished my university degree and took up a full-time role as an engineer building railway lines in Sydney. The hours were long, sometimes including weekend and night shift work; furthermore, the project had only two more years to run, and I wasn't sure where my next job would be.

This was when I became fully determined not to fall into the traditional trap of working until I was 65. I think it had a lot to do with my nostalgia for the good times I'd had when travelling and working different jobs, before being trapped in my full-time engineering role.

I began to visualise what my life might look like in 40 years if I stayed this course. The fact that I didn't have a passion for engineering meant I wasn't that happy with my prospects. However, I was young and didn't have any other burning desires (except for travel), so for now I didn't really see any other option. I had also just met my future wife, Mina, and I was happy in my personal life. Why rock the boat?

Well, there'd be no book if I'd stuck with that way of thinking! Later that year I began sniffing around the property market again.

Taking the first step

A year later, in 2010, I was 23—and it was time. I wasn't going to let the bank reject me again, so I took in a hard-earned deposit of $60 000 and we finally got a loan approved by the bank.

Our first property was in Sutherland—yes, in my own Sydney backyard. It was a freestanding house with a granny flat and cost $480 000. We did a 90 per cent lend with ANZ. Because the granny flat and the house were rented separately, there were essentially two rental incomes on the property, producing a total rent of $660 a week. This income was enough to cover all the interest, maintenance, insurance, rates and other holding costs. In fact, after all those costs we were left with over $200 a week cash as a passive income. So, in a way, we had just bought ourselves a $10 000 per annum pay rise!

At the time, all the media outlets were producing regular doomsday articles predicting an imminent 30 to 40 per cent price drop for the Sydney property market. I won't lie: as a first-time investor I was spooked by these articles, but I decided to push on through as I knew the fundamentals of the property were strong. I was still getting a return on investment via cash flow, and this made me feel a lot better about entering the market for the first time. It also helped that I had a strong mindset around building a large portfolio, and I still do. Today, even with the recent falls, that Sutherland property is valued at over $1 million, roughly $600 000 more than we paid for it. I'm glad I didn't listen to the media doomsayers, because had I bought into the property crash fear we would have lost a small fortune in opportunity costs.

At the time I didn't yet know how the media uses 'clickbait' articles to sell papers. One way around that was self-education. So I read thousands of property comments and opinions in web forums, and I devoured every property book I could find, though few of them discussed commercial property. The more I read, the more I realised that buying and holding for the long term was the true path to financial freedom. What helped me in

2010 was that most people were fearful of price falls and had a negative mindset, which meant we could buy property at a great price. It wasn't so very different from what we saw in 2020 with COVID-19.

We bought our second property in Maroubra in 2012 through ANZ with 85 per cent leverage and no lenders' mortgage insurance (LMI). It was a unit, and its value rose $300000 in just four years. Admittedly, lending was a little easier back then, and at the time we were creating equity while maintaining cash flow. So Mina and I were quickly thinking about our third property.

A lightbulb moment

In the European summer of 2013, while we were in Greece, I was thinking about what was waiting for me back in Australia. Mainly a new job in Port Macquarie that required us to relocate. It was a large and potentially stressful role that encompassed responsibility for three separate business units (quarries, logistics and concrete production)—a very big role for someone my age. Sure, it was an exciting opportunity, but I was moving away from family and friends to progress my career—which, as I've said, I was never passionate about.

I've found that when I'm on holiday I can often think more clearly and deeply, and right then I knew something was wrong. Something was missing. My mind turned to our two investment properties: the highly positively geared dual-income house in Sutherland and the slightly negatively geared property in Maroubra, both in Sydney. Both had produced significant capital growth over the past few years. In fact, we had made more money from these two investments than from my entire salary over the same period. Even better was the cash flow we were receiving on top of the growth. At the time, the Sutherland property was producing a net income of nearly $300 a week. We'd owned it for three years and in that time we were able to increase the rent another $100 per week since we first purchased it.

As I was sitting on that Greek beach, it hit me. What if I could somehow purchase another five properties similar to the one in Sutherland, *but outside Sydney*? Sydney was getting expensive even for renters, and the numbers weren't stacking up to buy a big family home either. For our first two properties we had restricted our search to our own neighbourhood. What about investing further afield?

I worked out that I could earn more than $7500 a month clear plus capital growth if we bought another five properties elsewhere in Australia. This figure would constantly grow over time as well. And we'd have enough passive income to live for the rest of our lives in Greece, Bali or somewhere else with lower living costs. We could have a comfortable retirement, all achieved through property. Sounded like paradise compared with working in a mine until my late sixties!

It had taken me three years from buying that first property to reach this 'aha' moment, and it cemented forever my commitment to investing in property. Without a passive income, there can be no retirement *unless you sell off your assets.* And property investment in areas outside of the familiar would be a great vehicle to create that passive income. Furthermore, by setting a solid goal, we would have something concrete to work towards. With that in mind, our first goal was to replace Mina's income, and the goal after that was to replace mine.

In 2013, Mina and I relocated to Port Macquarie for my demanding new job. Not long after the move we were able to buy another property for around $450 000, using an 80 per cent loan and 20 per cent cash we'd saved from working. This next purchase has always been one of my favourite properties: four units on one title with a price of $425 000. It was far from my familiar patch in Sydney, and almost everyone I talked to about the property at the time expressed concerns: it was too regional, it wasn't going to attract any capital growth, the banks wouldn't like it, and the tenants would give you too much trouble. And on.

But the numbers worked. At the time, the average yield in this area was about 4 to 4.5 per cent, yet this small unit block was showing a gross yield of 9.8 per cent generated from four separate tenants each paying $200 a week! It was clear that the cash flow would be better than anything else in town. I also knew that the property would be easily relet, because it was one of the cheapest places to rent in the town and just 300 metres from the beach.

Finding tenants fast was always important for me, as income security was what I was investing for. So the length of time needed to find tenants is one of the most significant factors. This is particularly important in commercial investing, so all our experiences with residential properties were laying the foundations for our commercial property debut.

Our fourth property search started quickly. We had our Port Macquarie unit block (bought for $425 000) revalued at $500 000 six months later. This meant we had more equity to spend, on top of the savings we had put away.

This fourth purchase was almost a replica of that small unit block, but it was on the Gold Coast. Again, it was very high yielding (it had a gross yield of about 11 per cent). So once the outgoings and the mortgage were taken out, we were left with another $18 000 in passive income from the purchase. Adding this $18 000 to the other incomes generated from our other properties brought our total property passive income to around $65 000.

The fifth purchase was another unit block on the Gold Coast. For the deposit we used equity from our Maroubra property, which had grown in value. We bought this at roughly $40 000 below market value, which was another good source of equity down the track. This slightly older unit block was clearing $16 000 per annum in passive income between the three units.

You'll have noticed that I always look at the income *after* mortgage costs for these properties, as this gives me the actual workable income. For many others, the costs and the mortgage are a secondary part of the equation. We also started strata titling the property, which would create more equity and free up another deposit for a rainy day.

Our sixth property was an undervalued, slightly older house in Brisbane. This was sitting on a good-sized block that could lend itself to upgrades down the track. We paid $270 000 for the house when all others on the street were selling for about $50 000 more. The yield was around 6 per cent. After all costs this left us with another $5000 per annum surplus in cash flow.

Our seventh property was another unit block in Port Macquarie: five units on one title that we strata titled for a profit. We bought the Port Macquarie unit block using equity from one of our Gold Coast properties plus equity from our first property in Sutherland and some cash savings for stamp duty.

Finance was more difficult for this property. It was one of our more stressful purchases due simply to our running out of available funds for the purchase. We also had difficulties keeping the bank on time for settlement. It was a painfully slow process, and it felt like the bank was looking for reasons not to grant us the loan. Also, the agent had multiple backup buyers lined up, which meant we were going to lose the property if we couldn't get the loan approved in time. Fortunately, it all worked out. The bank wanted a larger deposit, so at the last minute I had to obtain a personal loan to cover a cash shortfall.

The purchase price was $710 000, and after strata titling it the property was revalued at $1.2 million. Although it was more stressful than the others, it was one of our best deals. The equity we created by buying it at such a good price led to further purchases down the track.

Our eighth, ninth, tenth and eleventh properties were created by splitting up the seventh property into five units, all on separate titles. This freed up a lot of equity, which allowed us to go on a little shopping spree.

The 12th purchase was another unit block, this time in the regional NSW town of Cooma. You can tell we were becoming a little obsessed with unit blocks! By now we had found it to be a winning formula, as commercial property has since become. It was four units on one title, for which we paid $195 000, and it would be revalued at $300 000 just two years later.

Using the profits from our capital growth, we then bought several houses in Queensland and South Australia, and at this point things started to move more quickly for us.

My approach has always been to study, study and study some more. I reviewed several hundred properties online every week, year after year, which added up to more than 100 000 properties over the years. I would enter the best of these properties with all their attributes and numbers in spreadsheets for comparison. When I was looking to buy, I would review them, assessing every cost and risk. When I was ready to purchase, I knew every unit block in the country that was for sale. To help the decision making, I'd list all the investment strengths and weaknesses along with all the numbers on the properties. This register would include outgoings, renovations required, potential rent, upsides, street quality and even appearance. It all helped me grade and compare properties faster. We now use a similar system at Rethink Investing, which allows us to compare every commercial property on the market. It takes a team of us to handle the workload, but we know we're identifying the best deals available around the country at each specific price point.

When I started to realise there weren't enough good deals advertised online, I began doing letterbox drops to prospective properties to let them know I was willing to put in an offer on their property without the need for a real estate agent. I was doing everything I could to increase my chances of getting a good deal.

While putting a lot of time into my investing, I was also very consciously saving every dollar I could. I took on a lot of minor renovations myself; for example, I sanded floors and had a go at a kitchen. I was managing all our properties, which involved everything from advertising on Gumtree to tenant interviews to dealing with maintenance call-outs. Although it was a time-consuming exercise, it helped us save money faster and get to know our properties better.

Throughout this time I was also studying for an MBA and working full time. As I mentioned earlier, building our property portfolio didn't come easy. It took a lot of time and a *lot* of effort.

But back to the lightbulb moment. By concentrating on buying properties that produced good passive incomes and not being bound to any particular location, we made better investment decisions. It felt like we were growing a business, acquiring $5000 to $25 000 extra positive cash flow each time we bought a new property.

At just 26 years old, I was doing what it seemed like no-one else at the time was doing. I became obsessed! But I knew this was just the beginning. My goal was to create a passive income of $150 000 before I was 28, at which point we could decide never to work again if we chose. We were well on our way to achieving our plans.

The big pivot

By 2015, with Mina's mum unwell, as she'll explain later, we had moved back to Sydney from Port Macquarie. We'd enjoyed five years of successfully generating great returns from our residential property portfolio, but we'd started to run up against an obstacle: the yields were getting lower and lower. The residential market was getting tougher by the year because rents were not keeping up with the growth, which meant that replicating the quality residential investment deals we had once relied on to create income from positive cash flow was getting increasingly difficult.

The unit blocks on the market were not as high yielding either. For example, our early unit blocks were producing gross yields of 10 per cent. Now the best I could find was 6 to 6.5 per cent. The falling yields were due to the significant amount of capital growth that the unit block market had achieved over the previous few years. I guess this was to be expected as the yields couldn't stay that high forever. As more investors started targeting the same unit blocks I was, the prices grew. Over time the value was just not there anymore. So this effectively put an end to the unit block strategy that had been going so well. Which meant cash flow had to be found somewhere else.

At the same time I was forced to accept lower yields than I wanted to in my searches. I was also faced with several tenancy-related issues in my residential properties. One of the drawbacks of owning many rental properties is there are always issues to deal with, especially if you are buying at the cheaper end of the rental spectrum. For example, drug addicts at our first property would drop syringes into the toilet, which kept blocking. Not surprisingly, no plumber wanted to go around to my place after a while!

In another we had to have the police intervene in a domestic violence situation. We also faced additional costs from property damage and unanticipated vacancies. Property investing isn't much fun when you're dealing with tenants coming and going all the time. But more about that later in the book.

At one point I was personally managing nine properties in two different states without using rental managers. It was all taking up a hell of a lot of my time, and I was doing it all outside business hours.

The way I saw it, we had two options. We could persevere in the residential property, where the cash flow was starting to head south. Or we could look again 'outside our own backyard' — to the commercial market.

In my search for numbers that stacked up, I had started to research commercial properties. To my surprise, the numbers and yields were far greater than anything I had seen in the residential markets. I couldn't believe it! To an obsessive number cruncher like me, it was a potential gold mine. It was almost too good to be true. How and why was this possible? I needed to make sense of it all, because if it was true, we could surely fast-track our goals and retire even earlier than we'd first thought!

We wanted faster results, and I became convinced that to achieve this meant moving into the commercial property market. But before I did, I needed to learn everything I could about this new sector. I researched all aspects thoroughly, from office space to retail to industrial, and even the development side of commercial property. After around 12 months spent reading and learning, my objective was to find a property I believed could withstand a recession. I wanted a high yield, a long lease, a solid trading history in a market that hadn't already boomed and preferably in an essential service industry.

When I asked others for their opinions, to my surprise it seemed like everyone was against investing in commercial property. Everyone. Family, friends, brokers, advisers—none of them seemed to really understand the commercial property market at all. I asked them if they personally owned commercial property, but all I got back was crickets! Disappointed but undeterred, I decided to back myself, as I was now convinced that commercial property was potentially a very profitable market to get into.

Up to this point, we had still only bought residential properties. You'll read about our first commercial purchase in Part I. It was the start of my obsession with commercial property.

Fast forward a couple of years to 2016 and we had achieved our goal of replacing both of our salaries. As related in the preface, I was still only 28 at the time and we had grown our portfolio to 25 properties in both residential and commercial when we decided to take off on that six-month trip to Europe to celebrate our success. It was an exciting feeling, but it also made us think about taking what we had done to the next level.

At the time we owned four commercial properties that produced a whopping $207 000 net income. The mortgage cost was around $75 000 for the commercial loans. So our income had jumped $132 000 from these four commercial properties alone. This meant our passive income sat at just under $300 000 from our total portfolio. We realised that we wanted to spend our future helping others achieve their own wealth goals—and so our professional business, Rethink Investing, was born.

Today, through our business, we have helped clients purchase more than $1 billion of Australian real estate, most of it commercial property. And the numbers continue to grow every month. More and more people are realising the value of commercial property as a high-performing asset class. I strongly believe it's where cash flow can still be found in today's markets.

Mina's story

I have always dreamed of a life in which I can open my computer to work when I *want* to, rather than when I *have* to. But it took a long time and a lot of hard work to get to that point. And, like Scott, it all started with the positive cash flow mindset in my DNA.

While Scott and I share the same approach to money today, our property journeys to get there have been very different. I can narrow mine down to two key principles: sacrifice and saving, both learned from my parents.

Family values

My mother came to Australia when she was about 10 years old with her family from Egypt. She was a hard worker and saver. From a young age she would help her mum and dad with rent, groceries and bills and however else she could. She was also an opportunist. She found work wherever she could, which gave her the skills to work in many fields, from admin to retail. Above all she was a fantastic writer. Nothing would stop my mum from getting where she needed to be.

My father came from a family of 12 on the small Greek island of Kos. He dropped out of school at 12 years old to work in the family business, becoming a butcher like his father and grandfather before him.

His family was very poor. All 12 children slept in one room in their big, two-bedroom home. The aftermath of World War II was hard on Kos, and all members of the family had to work. Shoes, food and especially sweets (my father used to look at chocolates in a store window and rub his belly imagining he was eating them) were hard to come by in his village.

When he arrived in Australia he couldn't speak a word of English, but he was determined to make a better life. He found work as a butcher and sent the first few dollars he earned back to his parents in Greece. He worked day and night to earn a living in Australia, sending much of his hard-earned cash back to his family while also building his own nest.

The lure of property first surfaced after he met my mother, when he declared he wouldn't marry her until he could put a roof over her head. He made that happen in 1982, buying his first property, a three-bedroom unit in Kingsford, Sydney, where he lived.

When the recession hit in the early nineties, my father decided a change was needed. By 1992, with the economy recovering, he was presented with an opportunity to build his own unit block with shopfronts back home on Kos—and he was bitten by the property bug. He decided to move us all (my mum, my eight-month-old brother and me, then three years old) back to Greece while he pursued this business opportunity. The plan was for us to live there for five years then return to Australia.

He built the unit block and each of his three brothers took ownership of one shop and unit plus a block of land at the rear. He then took over the family butchery business with one of his brothers and worked day and night to create a comfortable life for his family. We ended up living in Greece for 10 years.

My father had approached investing by asking himself two key questions: What is the point of investing without purpose? Why not make your money work for you? From a young age, these ideas were embedded in me as I learned by watching my parents and taking note of my surrounding environment. Already the seeds were sown in the way I would come to think about investing.

During the 1980s and '90s, another global health crisis, mad cow disease, made its appearance in Europe, destroying many butchery businesses, and Dad was forced to pivot again. He decided to build more units on the island and he also bought land. Today some of his properties still provide produce for the shop where he now works. My dad, the simple butcher, made a new life as a restaurant/café/bar owner. Entrepreneurship was in his blood!

To a young girl, witnessing all this was hugely formative. Dad still tells me, 'You should always have money in your pocket. If you don't, then don't go out until you have some you can spend and some you can leave for a rainy day!' He would also say, 'Why not invest your money but make a profit after costs? To be successful, your mind needs to be sharp to understand how money will work for you.'

I can see how his mindset came to influence me even back then. For example, I can remember at age 10 puzzling how I was to afford a chocolate bar I particularly wanted. I decided to sell my sticker collection one by one until I had enough to buy the chocolate bar with a little left over to set aside for a rainy day. To achieve this, I had to make sure I sold each sticker for a little more than I paid for it, which meant I made a small profit so I would have to work maybe only half as hard to get my second chocolate bar.

I loved the feeling of accomplishment when handing over my carefully earned cash, knowing I had also made a profit from the proceeds of my sticker collection. I loved the work side of it, but more than that I loved the reward! Just as I had learned from my dad.

His business mind, his ability to teach me the value of family, and the importance of saving to achieve independence, still inspire me every day. The way he rose above his humble beginnings to become an experienced businessman and property investor is something I've always admired and appreciated. I count myself very lucky to be my father's daughter.

My mother, too, gave me the opportunity for a better life in Australia with good schools and a secure roof over my head. They were always looking for a good deal. When we moved to Randwick, after living with my grandmother, Dad wanted to upgrade to a larger home to accommodate our growing family. He'd bought it for about $450 000—we lived there for six years—and sold it for $660 000.

He found a larger home in Pagewood, in Sydney's southern suburbs, though it needed a lot of work. When we found out it was a distressed sale (the owner had left suddenly to go overseas and needed a quick sale), we realised what a gold mine it was! By then I was 18 and had started to see things through their investors' eyes. And I liked it! We could see the house wasn't worth much, but we could buy the land, knock it down and rebuild, then one day sell it for a good profit.

We ended up buying it for about $714 000 and living in a rental while building the new home for about $450 000. Five years later we resold it for $1.8 million. I'd learned my first lesson as a kid selling stickers, but now I was starting to think like a professional investor!

A mother's love

Through my mother I learned to appreciate life in a different way. When I was 12 years old she contracted ovarian cancer. We moved back to Australia so she could receive the cancer treatment she needed through Australia's superior healthcare system. Dad stayed on in Greece, so we moved into my grandmother's place, all of us sleeping in one room. My brother had a mattress on the floor, while Mum and I shared the queen-size bed. Dad would visit for a few months every year then return to Greece to work. When Mum was well enough and I had started school, we moved into our own place, living in one of my parents' investment properties in Randwick, in Sydney's eastern suburbs. We'd also travel to Greece to visit Dad when we could.

Over the years I saw what cancer could do to a person. Mum was my rock, my inspiration; her example always encouraged me to do better and to be strong. She battled her illness for 16 years, suffering eight recurrences, a full hysterectomy and multiple chemotherapy courses. She was only 39 when she was first diagnosed, which was unusually young for this disease.

After Scott and I relocated to Port Macquarie, every weekend for two years I travelled back to Sydney to spend time with her. I could feel in my bones that every moment spent with her counted, because I didn't know how much longer her poor frail body could survive. When we found out she didn't have many more months to live, we decided to move back to Sydney to stay close to her. We quickly packed up our lives in Port Macquarie and I quit my job. Back in Sydney, for a time Scott and I lived on a mattress on the floor. We only had a few cups, a mini fridge and basic necessities, but we were close to family.

By then we had 18 investment properties under our belt. Quite simply, if we hadn't had those properties, which were accruing enough passive income to replace our salaries, I would never have been able to spend as much time with my mum as I did, especially during those last few months.

I am so grateful that I was able to go every day to help her shower, to hold mini-parties in the hospital and even host a mock-wedding ceremony with my celebrant in the hospital. The staff knew Mum so well that we threw a separate party there in her honour, knowing she wasn't going to be able to make it to our wedding.

She passed away on September 14, 2015.

Mum taught me two of my biggest life lessons: that life is precious, and that it should never be taken for granted. Life's too short not to enjoy it, so I made a commitment to live it to the fullest.

Her courage and persistence taught me to never give up on what you want and what you believe in. And that the most important thing is to stay true to yourself and to act with honesty and passion, without worrying what others do around you. My mum and dad had no time for lies and deceit. Honesty and humility, and always doing the right thing, can take you a long way. 'Patience is a virtue,' she always said. 'You'll see, good things will come your way.'

Investment lessons

From my parents I learned the value of clearly understanding what's important to you and doing what it takes to work towards it. That's what still drives me today.

I learned that the main purpose of earning money was to allow you to live life to the fullest, because you never know when it may end. So I said to myself, how can I do that? Again, it was Mum and Dad who prompted me to find the answer in property investing.

When our property investing journey began, we were like everyone else just starting out in the residential property market. We did our research, calculated our return and made sure we had a cash flow profit after paying all our expenses. Dad's early lessons were always in my mind: Why not make your money work for you? What is the point of investing without purpose? No matter what I invested my money in, these ideas shaped my thought patterns.

Dad also taught me to think of investing as like building a business. Whenever you spend money on a business, you expect a return via cash flow profits in the short term. Investing in property should be no different. Another key idea was that while you should work 'hard', you should also work 'smart'. Once again, I asked myself how I could get there.

As I mentioned, our first financial goal was to replace my income, which would enable me to spend time with my mum and to enjoy the time I wanted when I wanted with my family. Our ultimate plan was to replace both our salaries, giving us freedom and independence, and eliminating the need to work for a salary all our lives. I soon realised I needed a plan with set goals that would give me the fuel to accomplish them. A big part of this was making sure I had cash in my pocket each year after all costs. This is my positive cash flow mindset.

Unlike my parents, I always struggled with the idea of buying an investment property that was negatively geared. If we purchased a property and found it hard to pay off, then how could we gain the flexibility of being able to travel each year? From very early on I knew the importance of prioritising good cash flow investments over those that couldn't produce a passive income.

All these lessons inspired our first property purchase in Sutherland. I remember when Scott came to me and asked me what I thought about it. It was a run-down dual occupancy home, with lots of work and maintenance needed. If it was to be our principal place of interest, it was basically a knock-down rebuild.

But we saw what it was rented for, how much our lending capacity was and what the loan repayments would be after all costs. When we ran the numbers it offered a good return, and the location was booming.

Our second purchase, the Maroubra property, was partly based on emotion, mainly because it would be our primary residence. It was negatively geared and cost us more to live in than it returned financially, but at the time it was a place to live more than an investment.

Starting Rethink Investing

We then moved to Port Macquarie for the job that Scott couldn't refuse, which would give us the kickstart we needed in investing. At the time my job prospects were limited, and despite having a strong background in politics and journalism, specialising in advertising and national operations, I went back to my roots in retail.

As a young girl, retail had been my go-to. I always wanted my mind to be active, I never stopped looking for challenges, and I was never afraid of hard work. My first job was at a store called GoLo. At the tender age of 14½, I was the youngest employee in the store, but in no time I rose from stacking the shelves to managing the tills and customer complaints and closing up shop. Within six months I was made supervisor.

Moving to Port Macquarie taught me some valuable lessons, among them to never forget where you're from—your roots. Eventually I had an opportunity to complete studies in human resources, which proved very helpful when establishing Rethink Investing. I also worked for a council in their communications department, and for a financial planner in administration and operations.

Having to learn and juggle so many different roles due to the lack of job prospects in a regional town had boosted my skill set and increased my knowledge of property investing. That's when we purchased our third property in Port Macquarie, the unit block with four two-bedroom units on one title. This was our highest yielding investment to date. It produced over $18 000 per annum after all costs, including the mortgage.

When my mother passed away and we returned to Sydney, I had no job and Scott was already buying properties for friends and family on the side. I thought, why not help start to build a brand for our new business? I began working from a mattress on the floor. It was a new and interesting challenge. I shared everything I learned and wanted to help others do the same. I started to build the back-end and core of the business.

Based on my experience in operations, advertising, human resources and administration, I began to build what you physically see as Rethink Investing today. I started from scratch, having never done anything like it before, so it was a major learning experience. I knew it would change my life forever. While Scott was helping clients buy their properties to build their own portfolio, I was creating a database, building a website, designing marketing materials, introducing accounting software—you name it and I did it.

Over the next few years we had a lot of success buying high-yielding residential real estate. Our successes with the Port Macquarie unit block led us to chase similar high yielding investments. Eventually, though, as Scott has described, it began to get much more difficult to achieve the yields we needed in residential. Ultimately this led us to look over the fence at commercial real estate. And let me tell you it was an absolute game changer!

As you'll read at the start of Part I, our first small commercial investment generated a whopping $46 800 passive income after all mortgage costs and outgoings. We were living in Sydney, where the cost of living was pretty high, but that one property paid our rent and we still had a surplus! That's the power of commercial property.

Purchasing properties with this level of cash flow return, we were not relying solely on capital growth to profit. This took much of the risk out of the investments for us. For example, if we didn't get capital growth every year on a property, that was okay because we were getting our profits month to month from the cash flow. I know now that I could never have bought a property in any other way to facilitate what I wanted in my own life and for my family.

I never took money for granted and was propelled forward by a determination to make my parents proud of me. I knew to think beyond our backyard and learn from the experiences of others, especially their reverses.

Today, as we strive to help others achieve their dreams and ambitions, just as we did when we started out, I never forget the freedom that property investing has provided for me and my family, and the lesson that as things change, you can change too.

Now let's get started!

MOVING BEYOND YOUR BACKYARD

Often when someone tells me not to do something, I immediately want to know why not?—well, when it relates to investing, at least. I take calculated risks and I thrive on challenging the status quo. After all, if you follow what everyone else does, you get the same result, right? I always wanted a little more than the average result. Negativity in investing choices is something I've faced a lot throughout my investing career. Yet year after year it has continued to change our lives for the better.

We encountered this negativity in spades when we decided to move into commercial property. It was 2015, and we had already built up a considerable portfolio of residential property. As we've mentioned, after several successful years purchasing residential houses and unit blocks, the cash flow returns were getting tighter and tighter.

For example, the unit blocks we purchased in 2014 had gross yields of over 9 per cent, which was a great return! Eighteen months later the unit block market had grown in value, but the rents hadn't. This meant that if we had put the unit blocks on the market, they could have been sold for a 6 per cent gross yield. This yield compression was fantastic for the capital growth of our existing properties, but the opportunity to find other good deals like this had all but dried up. We just knew there had to be other options beyond residential housing, and we really wanted to do things differently from how they had been done before.

But before moving on to commercial property we made one last-ditch effort to find another good-value unit block. I printed off a stack of letters that read:

> To the owner of the building,
>
> My name is Scott O'Neill. I'm a local investor looking to purchase a unit-block like this property. I'm willing to pay above market value for your property if you wish to sell it directly to me. Also, by selling to me directly, you will not have to pay a sales agent commission – making this a more profitable sale for you. If you would like to discuss this further with me, please reach out to me via . . .

Over the following month I dropped off some 200 of these letters up and down the coast from Wyong to Byron Bay. Guess how many responses we got? Not many! And even those simply replied along the lines of, 'We are not interested in selling at this point of time, but we will keep you in mind for when we wish to sell.'

This was the last straw. I was now ready to learn everything I could about commercial property investment. For the next few months I taught myself everything I could on the topic. I started by asking other investors about their experience with commercial property. I heard many amazing success stories, from multimillionaires in the 1970s who owned large parts of industrial suburbs all the way down to small-time investors who purchased a single retail shop. The more I spoke to people, though, the more I realised that not many people did this. And it was hard to find anyone who had started investing in commercial, especially younger investors. It seemed clear to me that in Australia the focus for investors was almost exclusively on residential, while commercial investing seemed like a forgotten part of the property investment world.

As I spoke to more experienced commercial investors, a common theme began to emerge. Once they had purchased their first commercial property, they never went back to the residential market. This was due to two main factors: higher cash flow and better tenants. The cash flow could help us hit our goals, and better tenants would give us less hassle. Residential cash flow was no longer enough for us to reach our income goals, and at the time we were dealing with a few bad tenants in some of the houses we'd bought years earlier.

The next part of my self-education was to start identifying the types of commercial properties I wanted to invest in. Again, I did my research. I had read everything I could on commercial property, spoken to dozens of agents, banks, brokers and property experts, and had all my finance lined up, so I finally felt ready to jump in. Importantly, my mindset was prepared, and although I was nervous about lacking the expertise, I was hungry to start learning how to mitigate the risks and reap the returns.

—*Scott*

OUR FIRST COMMERCIAL PROPERTY PURCHASE

We had bought our first residential property just after the GFC, so we were drawn to properties that were likely to hold their value in tough economic times. For example, our Sutherland house was near a train station and had two tenancies (a three-bedroom house plus a two-bedroom granny flat with its own entry). Our theory was that no matter how bad the economy, people would always need a cheap place to rent, and a train station ensured the property would always be convenient to those renters.

We applied the same thinking to our first commercial property. We decided that we wanted to purchase a cheap food-related business in a market that was not at its peak.

Later in 2015, after months of searching, we finally found a commercial property that ticked all the boxes. It was two shops on two separate titles, one a mini supermarket and the other a fish and chip shop. Both had been in business for about 20 years. It was in Perth, so we couldn't have picked a more geographically remote location if we tried! But, confident that the numbers would work, we decided to go for it.

Not that we received any votes of confidence from the people closest to us. Everyone, including family members, told us, 'Don't do it. You're crazy!' 'It's too risky', 'It's not the right time.' We saw this negativity as stemming from a fear of the unknown. Commercial property isn't as 'relatable' as residential, and to many people it seems more uncertain and complex than residential. But we'd heard it all before, and we weren't going to let the fearmongering turn us away. It just made us hungrier by confirming that this was something not many people were onto, which made us like the idea even more.

The fish and chip shop came with a solid three-year lease, but the supermarket had only 11 months left on the lease. From our due diligence, we knew that both tenants had long, secure trading histories and we could see that this one never missed a payment. For us, taking on the 11-month lease was a calculated risk, and in the end it paid off when we renegotiated the expiring lease into a 5+5-year lease. Also, the market in Perth was in a state of decline, which presented us with a better opportunity to secure the property for a good price. Another tick.

Here were the pros and cons of the property:

Pros:

- Two incomes, which spread the risk and reduced the likelihood of a total vacancy.

- Both businesses had been around for 20 years. The prospects looked good for continuing stability long into the future.

- Perth was a market that had suffered greatly in recent times, yet these properties were still renting out steadily.

- The price was good and the net yield was about 7.5 per cent.

Cons:

- The supermarket had only 11 months left on a five-year lease. This represented a big risk.

- The property needed work to bring it up to date.

- Our mortgage broker initially recommended that we stick to residential lending, as they had less experience with commercial finance.

Now, this is where it got a little tricky. Once we found the property the doubts crept in. Was this really where we should sink our hard-earned money?

First, our mortgage broker advised us to walk away from the deal. She warned that the interest rate was going to be higher; sticking with residential would have been much easier. Given that she was part of a residential specialist mortgage brokerage, this advice should not have come as a surprise. After all, the commercial sector was outside the scope of their core business. From our experience, a residential broker will generally prefer to write a residential loan than a commercial one. In our business, we see multiple clients each month wanting to invest in commercial property. Our firm advice is always to work with a mortgage broker who specialises in commercial loans. It's all about having the right professional team around you, a key point we'll cover later in the book.

Next, Scott asked a Perth local he'd met and become mates with while travelling. He mentioned the area where the property was situated and asked what it was like. As he was a bit older and didn't know Scott was already an experienced investor, he immediately sounded the alarm, arguing strongly against the deal, insisting the Perth market was 'terrible'. This made us very nervous! After all, the mortgage broker had already expressed much the same view.

Family members were also discouraging. Surely we'd bought enough properties, they argued. Of course, they worried about our taking risks they wouldn't take themselves.

Our plan attracted negative opinions from all sides, until we reached the point where we were seriously considering putting it in the too-hard basket.

So why did we eventually go ahead anyway?

There was one blindingly positive factor we could not get past: the numbers were just too good! After all mortgage repayments, land tax, maintenance, insurance, rental management, rates and so on, we were still left with an annual passive income of $46 800 a year. That's $900 a week for doing nothing at all!

We had by then moved back to Sydney. With our commercial investment netting $900 a week as an income ($46 800/52 weeks = $900), we could pay 100 per cent of our rent at the time. Which was great because we were living in the expensive Eastern Suburbs of Sydney effectively for free due to this passive income. For Scott, a former engineer and the son of an accountant, numbers will always speak louder than opinions. And the numbers won out.

So we decided to proceed, but we had to get finance and sort out the contract quickly. The problem was that three days later we were due to fly to Japan for three weeks. Mina's mum had recently passed away, and we were looking forward to a much-needed holiday. We did everything we could with the loan paperwork, but eventually we ran out of time and accepted that we would have to sort the rest out from Japan.

On the date contracts were to be exchanged, we were in a hotel in Tokyo. Scanning 40 pages of a contract in the hotel lobby at three in the morning wasn't easy, but we knew we had to beat another buyer to the punch. Finally we got the job done and the contracts exchanged. We then had 14 days to complete a valuation, get full loan approval, and arrange building and pest reports. We ended up needing 21 days before the contract went unconditional, but the agent was happy to grant us that week's extension. It was a stressful ride, and we were unnerved by feelings of buyer's remorse, but we did it. And once we'd settled we started collecting rent.

We were commercial property owners!

Eleven months later we successfully pulled off another great value-adding play: we secured a much stronger lease with the supermarket tenant, having negotiated a new five-year lease with a 4 per cent increase, which the bank looked on very favourably. We bought the property for $620 000, renting for $46 800 a year, with the tenants paying all the outgoings.

Essentially, we had taken an average asset and turned it into a much more secure one simply by lengthening the lease. This added about $100 000 to the value, proving to us that commercial property can enjoy equity uplift, security and high cash flow. Since then we have purchased another seven commercial properties, taking our total to nine. It has been a game changer, to say the least. We did it by not only looking beyond our expertise in residential, but also geographically beyond what we were familiar with. We would never have secured such a positive result by investing $620 000 in Sydney.

We had made sure we had everything lined up and knew exactly what we were getting ourselves into. Once we had our first commercial property in the bag, we were on our way.

WHAT COMMERCIAL PROPERTY IS (AND ISN'T)

Despite our many years of investing experience, it has taken us a long time to understand what commercial property is and isn't. There's no point in investing your hard-earned money if you don't really 'get' how it works and how you can make money from it. So let's dive right in so you can really appreciate what we love so much about this investment vehicle.

What it is

Commercial property can be defined as any property that is zoned or used solely for business purposes. It may include shopping centres, strip malls, hotels, retail stores, warehouses, restaurants, industrial spaces, farms, office buildings, childcare centres, service stations, data centres, even vacant lots that have been designated as commercial by the local government. They are the buildings you see every day as you walk around your neighbourhood. Just as everyone needs a place to live, most of us need a place to work.

And just so you know, you can't build a business on a residential property or a home on a commercial property. This is because owners or builders of commercial properties must meet certain standards when constructing a business, from the style and specifications of the building to the number of parking spaces provided. Councils also have different zoning and regulations that must be adhered to. They also might have different tax rates compared with other types of properties.

Commercial properties can be divided into categories. There are hundreds of different options available, and choosing the right property and then the right tenant is often the most difficult part of starting your investing journey.

The key asset types are as follows.

Industrial

Industrial properties include heavy manufacturing, light assembly and warehousing. They are used to manufacture, process or store goods, and include factories, workshops and research facilities. Industrial properties can range in size from a small workshop of 50 square metres up to facilities of 200 000 square metres or more.

They generally provide higher yields than retail or other commercial investments, and also have longer lease periods due to the specialised nature and fit-out of the facilities required by tenants. In most cases they are the cheapest type of commercial property per square metre. They're usually relatively large, and have often been reconfigured to accommodate heavy machinery. Frequently their location is chosen for easy highway access. They may include office space too.

Often the specialised and often extensive nature of these fit-outs mean industrial tenants can make it costly to move properties. Generally, the larger the asset size, the smaller the tenant pool you have to choose from. But the benefit of larger warehouses is that the tenant needs to spend more money to move, which is likely to attract longer term tenants.

For example, a 20 000m^2 warehouse might attract a global logistics company. They will likely need to spend millions on fitting out the property so won't want to move on unless really necessary. On the other hand, the smaller the asset size, the larger the pool of tenants to choose from, so it can be easier to find a tenant.

Industrial leases generally vary from two to 10 years, but most sit in the three- to five-year range.

Retail

Retail properties are the sorts of commercial properties that most people will be most familiar with because we see and visit these businesses all the time. Used mainly to promote and sell consumer goods and services, they include supermarkets, department stores, specialty shops, convenience stores, pharmacies, hairdressers, hardware stores, liquored shops, food take away, discount stores, and so on. They range widely in size and may be home to one or hundreds of individual stores and businesses.

Retail properties can be broken into two types:

- *Discretionary spend reliant.* These types of retail properties are subject to shifts in consumer confidence and the wider economic climate, which means retail property owners often struggle with extended vacancy periods if the economy is not performing well. They may include travel agents, fashion stores, high-end restaurants and electronic goods stores.

- *Non-discretionary spend reliant.* These types of retail properties tend to perform consistently regardless of consumer confidence and wider economic performance. They include, for example, supermarkets, allied medical shopfronts, fast food outlets and hardware stores.

Retail leases generally vary from 12 months to 10 years, but most sit in the three- to five-year range.

Office

Office properties are found in both urban and suburban areas. Many of us work in them, so they're easy to identify. In large cities, they're typically found in high-rise buildings in the inner-city central business district (CBD), although many cities have smaller satellite CBDs in the form of business office parks or office campuses. Office properties are typically used by professional service providers.

One advantage of office investing is you are most often dealing with quality professional tenants. These may include global accounting firms, legal practices or government departments.

The downside of office investing is the sign-on costs. To encourage tenants to sign a long-term lease, office owners often need to offer incentives, which can take the form of a period of free rent, allowances for fit-outs, air-conditioning reconfiguration and internet services.

Incentives are a result of you needing to compete hard to secure a tenant, as they usually have a lot of options open to them, especially in the CBD. To date, this sector of the market was hit hardest by the COVID-19 pandemic as businesses chose flexible work-at-home arrangements to protect their employees from the virus. However, offices in suburban areas tended to perform better as social distancing requirements had less impact on smaller office blocks that were less dependent on lifts and less affected by public transport constraints.

Office leases, like retail, generally vary from 12 months to 10 years, but most sit in the two- to five-year range.

Boarding houses

A boarding house is defined as a house in which individual rooms are let out to short-term tenants, who share common areas such as kitchens, living rooms and often bathrooms. This classification does not include backpackers' accommodation, group homes, hotels or motels, seniors housing or serviced apartments. Given the multi-income nature of the investment, boarding houses can offer a comfortable transition for residential investors seeking cash flow returns on a commercial scale.

Keep in mind that this type of investment requires extensive and constant management owing to the transient nature of the tenant population. While the returns may look good on paper, the extra maintenance, management costs and vacancy issues can severely diminish the returns on the asset. Other types of commercial property will typically generate better returns than a boarding house.

Boarding house leases generally vary from one to 12 months but average around six months.

Unit blocks

A block of more than four units on one title can be classed as a commercial property. For years, banks have treated blocks of four or more units on one title as qualifying for a commercial loan, which increases the minimum deposit to approximately 30 per cent. The yields are also higher than standard single-occupancy residential properties, given the multiple incomes involved.

As with boarding houses, you will need to account for extra management and maintenance costs. A big difference, though, is that the units are fully self-contained, so they tend to attract longer term tenants. Unit blocks can often allow value-add plays such as strata titling. Strata titling involves changing the ownership structure of the building so you can turn a single title into a title on each unit. This means you can sell off the units individually, potentially at a higher per-square-metre rate.

Unit leases, like most standard residential agreements, are generally six or 12 months.

Land

Land zoned for commercial property typically falls into three categories: brownfield land, which is land once zoned for industrial use and that may be impaired; infill land, which is land that has been developed but is now vacant; and greenfield land, which is completely undeveloped land.

Land can be a useful investment if you are an owner-occupier looking to build a premises for your business, mainly because you can build to your own specs, laying out everything exactly as you wish.

In most cases there will be no holding income on vacant land, which rules it out for most investors. However, there are many examples where vacant land can be leased. For example, if you own land near a port, a logistics company may lease it to store shipping containers. In that case, rent will be payable, but at a lower per square metre rate than if it had a secure building.

Large-format retail properties

The large-format retail sector is typically represented by homemaker-type tenants as well as tenants previously represented in traditional department stores. Large-format retail now comprises a whopping 35 per cent of all retail floor space. Many of these types of properties are freestanding or part of a larger complex.

With this type of asset, you can expect long leases—three to 10 years in most cases—and tenants are very sticky once they are established. Prices start from around $2 million for standalone retail stores selling products such as furniture, floor coverings and other homemaker-type goods. Complexes are generally purchased by institutional investors, as prices are often north of $20 million.

Special purpose

Most other types of commercial property fall into the special purpose category. This includes car washes, self-storage buildings, theme parks, nursing homes, churches and marinas.

One of the most well-known special-purpose commercial property types is service stations. These are classed as special purpose as the property has a single use. Leases can be from five to 15 years and yields can be relatively favourable too. However, there are many things to consider before jumping into a fuel station asset, such as contamination and equipment maintenance. The key here is to know exactly what you are purchasing.

Mixed-use properties

These types of properties typically involve a shopfront with a residential unit upstairs. This provides the tenant with the opportunity to work and live in the same location. There's also the opportunity to rent out the unit separately in a multi-income scenario.

Something to consider is that they generally produce a lower yield because of the residential component of the property. As residential yields are lower, the residential floor space will bring down the overall net yield.

They can also be located in relatively expensive metro areas, where there's a lot of competition. This means vacancies can last longer and the unit itself isn't often as desirable to live in compared to units in residential areas, because it's located on a main road with other commercial properties. Prices for these properties generally start from $1 million.

It's important always to purchase the property for its leasable qualities first, before considering the strength of the tenant. One trick we always apply to asset selection is make sure you plan for a future vacancy. If you have confidence you will find a replacement tenant in a short period, then you have a quality property. If you are buying a property just because of a good tenant, this is going to put you at potential risk. Because what happens if that great tenant leaves and you're left with a long vacancy?

It's worth remembering that with commercial property you're interested in owning the property itself, not the business. The business has nothing to do with it, although it does play a part in the property selection and tenant process, because the right type of business with a secure, reliable tenant will help the longer term performance of your commercial asset.

What commercial property isn't

You know the story. Couple at auction keep bidding to push the price up. They have their hearts set on their 'forever home'. Couple ends up paying 20 per cent more than they had budgeted for, against another couple doing the same thing.

Say goodbye to the emotional pull of the heartstrings and the stress associated with buying residential property, because in commercial property the transaction revolves solely around cold, hard numbers and contracts, not people — and not emotion.

Another thing it isn't is completely unpredictable. By that we mean there is more certainty over tenants and the consistency of cash flow and even growth. Let's break this down.

Things are often a lot more predictable when dealing with commercial than with residential tenants. For example, one of the most significant reasons we were drawn away from the residential property market was inconsistency of net income, mostly because you are responsible for the outgoings and often tenants don't stay long term.

When it comes to maintenance (which is almost always covered by commercial tenants), in residential portfolios the uncertainty of having to cover extra costs can become an issue, especially when you own many residential properties. We often seem to be paying thousands every month in following up maintenance problems — from a leaking tap, faulty air conditioner or blocked toilet, to more major items such as leaking roofs, asbestos problems, replacing carpets and fences, and even structural issues. These items must be dealt with expeditiously and at your own expense. If your goal is to live off your rental income, uncertainty over maintenance costs can be a significant ongoing concern. This is not something commercial property investors need to deal with.

Lower quality tenants are another issue that residential investors find hard to avoid. Tenants generally sign six to 12-month leases and might stay longer, but rents are very cyclical. Compare this to commercial property, where rental increases are generally fixed at an annual 2.5 to 4 per cent. Commercial tenants have their own brand and reputation, so naturally you will find they are more stable tenants.

Growth, too, can be more predicable for commercial property. Why? Because rental growth is a good indicator of capital growth for commercial property. Residential is entirely market and sentiment driven.

Don't get us wrong, we love what residential property can do for you, but there comes a point in your investing career when commercial investments need to play a part. It's simply more profitable in terms of cash flow and also more scalable, so you can build faster and more easily.

WHAT YOU NEED TO KNOW FIRST

In a commercial property deal, the purchasing process is based on a simple mathematical formula plus market knowledge, which helps you value the correct yield for the offer. The offer is then turned into a contract, which is normally subject to a due diligence period. In this time window, you will have to review all the information on the property to verify if it's exactly as expected. This includes building and pest reports, lease reviews, outgoing checks, tenant checks and much more. If it all comes together as expected, great; if not, either walk away from the deal or renegotiate the price.

After settlement, one of the beauties of a commercial property deal is that you won't have to deal with the day-to-day minor items that are common in residential. This is because in most commercial lease documents, it's the tenant's responsibility to keep the premises fully functioning. This is another part of the due-diligence process. A solicitor or yourself must perform a full legal quality lease review to confirm assumptions, such as 'does the tenant cover maintenance?' or 'how much the rent should increase per annum?' and 'who pays for other outgoings such as land tax or rental management?'.

This bears repeating, because it's a game changer: *the tenant is responsible for the entire commercial space.* That means no more maintenance phone calls and the unpredictability around income that comes with it. Furthermore, at the end of the tenancy, the tenant must hand back the property in the same condition as it was at the beginning of the tenancy, minus the usual wear and tear. There are normally allowances in the lease to compensate the landlord for the costs associated with cleaning the property and returning it to its original condition. This is called the make good clause, which basically spells out the tenant's obligation to 'make good' the premises before handing back the keys. Understandably, it's the most commonly contentious provision in the contract, as these provisions are not often well understood.

Most commercial property tenants understand that the onus is on them to replace or repair anything on the site, while the owner's responsibility ends at providing a watertight building. The bonus here is that tenants can upgrade or refurbish the space themselves, and many do this because it helps them to market their business.

Another major point of difference is a commercial tenant is a business that has its own customer reputation to uphold, so by its nature it will be more self-sufficient.

We've now arrived at the best parts about commercial property investing. While we've already referred to some of these issues when discussing our personal experiences, here we'll review the most important things you need to know. These are the fundamentals of commercial property investing. With a good understanding of them, you can start to get your head around how and why it differs so much from the residential property market.

Essentially, you need to know about being cash flow positive and about yields. Let's break it down.

Cash flow positive

Put simply, commercial property investment is designed to be cash flow positive for investors. You may have heard this referred to as positive cash flow or positively geared — that is, it puts actual money in your pocket even when you have high debt levels.

Interestingly, positive cash flow investors are actually in the minority. In Australia, an incredible two out of three property investors claim a cash flow loss on their investments. Which means that the income you make from your property — rent — is less than your expenses, hence you make a loss. As some investors actively look to negatively gear property just to save tax, it becomes a tax position rather than a viable long-term strategy if you plan to retire anytime soon. The bigger aim of negative gearing is for the capital growth to offset the cash flow loss. But as we've said, we view losing month after month while relying on the prospect of future growth as an unacceptably slow road to success. And don't make the assumption that high-yielding properties can't also generate great capital growth.

As you can see in table 1, of the 1 811 175 individuals who reported to the ATO in 2018 as having an investment property, 1 213 595 of them (or two out of every three investors) recorded a loss on their rental income. The total value of these losses over the year was $13.285 billion. Negative gearing of investment properties allows owners to claim a tax deduction on these costs. The average annual loss for these property investors with negatively geared properties was $10 947, or $210.50 a week.

Table 1: taxation summary of rental properties

Gross rent	no. 1 788 690
	$30 730 421 999
Rent – interest deductions	no. 1 459 530
	$22 670 157 040
Capital works deductions	no. 734 565
	$1 920 663 564
Other rental deductions	no. 1 795 705
	$14 001 698 841
Net rent – profit	no. 597 575
	$5 422 999 805
Net rent – loss	no. 1 213 595
	–$13 285 087 251
Net rent	no. 1 811 175
	–$7 862 087 446

We recognise that you need more properties to make more money, but when it comes down to what the average Australian is doing, it's a different story again. Table 2 (overleaf) shows the average number of investment properties people own in Australia.

Table 2: individual investors' interest in rental properties

Property interests	2009-10 no.	2010-11 no.	%
1	1 239 959	1 284 852	72.8
2	307 514	318 295	18.0
3	92 834	96 991	5.5
4	33 501	34 967	2.0
5	14 141	14 555	0.8
6 or more	14 844	15 264	0.9
Total	1 702 793	1 764 9245	

What this table shows is that 90.8 per cent of investors never get past their second investment property, and that fewer than 1 per cent accrue more than six properties.

Why is this? Why don't many people seek to achieve financial freedom through property? From our experience, this is because they have:

- poor cash flow and lack of equity. Two out of three investors are negatively geared. The average annual loss for property investors with negatively geared properties was $10 947 or $210.50/week.
- no investment plan. They tend to:
    - buy based on emotion
    - buy in 'their own backyard'
    - follow the crowd rather than following markets closely
    - sell at the wrong time
    - select the wrong property.
- the wrong advice, whether from:
    - spruikers
    - friends and family
    - people with vested interests.

Over the years, we've seen many novice property investors adopt the mindset that they just need to put a property where they live. There isn't much thought beyond just finding something they are familiar with. This often ends up in a negative cash flow investment that doesn't grow as fast as they have hoped. In a way we view this type of invest as just trapping money in property and hoping for growth one day. Many of these investors simply do not prioritise the importance of deriving a good income from their investments. And they certainty are not trying to pick the best market in Australia for growth as well. They rationalise their poor returns by insisting that property is a 'long-term investment', which means they may see many years of poor results.

This mindset is one we were determined to avoid. We wanted to invest without it hurting our day-to-day lives, which the negative gearing method would have done. From day one we sought to make a fast return, which is why higher cash flow properties have always been more attractive to us. Cash flow positive — we were certain this was the only way anyone should invest.

Table 3 (overleaf) shows the cash flow at different debt levels (0–100 per cent debt) and at different interest rates available to commercial investors in 2021.

As you can see, a 7 per cent net yielding property, even at 100 per cent debt, at a 5 per cent interest loan still clears the investor $254 a week income before tax. Please note, we have included $5000 for depreciation, which is a conservative figure for the types of properties we target in this price range (warehouses, small medical suites and well-located retails shops). Commercial property has good depreciation benefits too, which help with your post-tax cash returns. More on that later.

Essentially, what this table shows is the key difference between residential and commercial property from an investor's point of view. In commercial property, your key goal is a high-yielding property that produces a consistent, uninterrupted income. Essentially, this is all you need in order to realise your retirement goal. And the type of asset and quality of tenant are important to achieving this result.

In residential property, the asset is typically negatively geared, meaning your income (rent) is less than your expenses so you make a loss. This is obviously not an ideal outcome, so why do people do it?

Table 3: cash flow returns calculations table

Price	$500 000	(net of outgoings)
Rent	$35 000	
Depreciation	$5000	
Rental management	5%	
Net yield	7.0%	

	Purchase price ($)	Annual rent ($)	Depreciation benefit ($)	Interest ($)	Rent mgt ($)	Cash return ($)
Cash buy	500 000	35 000	5000	0	1750	38 250
70 loan @ 3.5%	500 000	35 000	5000	12 250	1750	26 000
75 loan @ 3.5%	500 000	35 000	5000	13 125	1750	25 125
80 loan @ 3.5%	500 000	35 000	5000	14 000	1750	24 250
100 loan @ 3.5%	500 000	35 000	5000	17 500	1750	20 750
70 loan at 4%	500 000	35 000	5000	14 000	1750	24 250
75 loan at 4%	500 000	35 000	5000	15 000	1750	23 250
80 loan at 4%	500 000	35 000	5000	16 000	1750	22 250
100 loan @ 4%	500 000	35 000	5000	20 000	1750	18 250
70 loan @ 4.5%	500 000	35 000	5000	15 750	1750	22 500
75 loan @ 4.5%	500 000	35 000	5000	16 875	1750	21 375
80 loan @ 4.5%	500 000	35 000	5000	18 000	1750	20 250
100 loan @ 4.5%	500 000	35 000	5000	22 500	1750	15 750
70 loan @ 5%	500 000	35 000	5000	17 500	1750	20 750
75 loan @ 5%	500 000	35 000	5000	18 750	1750	19 500
80 loan @ 5%	500 000	35 000	5000	20 000	1750	18 250
100 loan @ 5%	500 000	35 000	5000	25 000	1750	13 250

One of the main reasons why people are more comfortable investing in residential real estate, aside from the fact that it is more familiar to them, is that they believe the capital growth prospects will be stronger, but this isn't always the case.

It's worth considering if many investors really understand how much growth they can expect over 30 years?

Table 4 shows median capital city house price changes over the past 30 years.

Table 4: median capital city house prices, 1990–2020

	1990 ($)	2020 ($)	Compound Annual Growth Rate (CAGR)
Sydney	194 000	950 000	5.44
Melbourne	131 000	732 500	5.91
Brisbane	113 000	541 000	5.36
Adelaide	97 200	470 000	5.39
Perth	101 125	480 000	5.33
Hobart	82 000	530 000	6.42
Darwin	101 500	465 000	5.20
Canberra	120 750	720 000	6.13

As you can see, the average house price growth in our capital cities is between 5.44 and 6.42 per cent. This level of growth is not too exciting, considering that the past 30 years, many would argue, have enjoyed the greatest growth for residential properties we will ever see.

Yields

This is another term you'll need to get to grips with. In commercial property, the yield is everything. It is the calculation you will use to work out if a commercial property is worth buying or not. You can also use the yield to compare with other yields in the sale area. For example, if you are putting in an offer on a property that shows a 7 per cent net return, but the market yield for that specific type of asset is averaging 6.5 per cent, then your 7 per cent yield looks relatively good from a valuation point of view (as long as the rent is at market value, of course).

A market yield can change over time too. Whether it goes up or down usually relates to good old-fashioned supply and demand and interest rates, but it's important to understand how it applies to commercial property.

Calculating net yield

It's important to understand how to calculate net yield, because this should be the foundation for every commercial property decision you will ever make. It's a formula we use in the office all the time:

Net income per annum (NIPA) = Total gross rent − Total outgoings

Net yield = (NIPA) / Purchase price × 100%

Let's break this down so you can fully understand how the formula works, starting with calculating the true net income per annum.

You're interested in buying an industrial property, and the purchase price is $1 million. The agent has listed the gross rent at $80 000 per annum and total annual outgoings at $7500. (This includes building insurance, maintenance and council rates. Please be careful to include all the outgoings, as agents often miss numbers. We'll talk about this later in the book.)

If we plug in the numbers, we can see that the rate of return is 7.25 per cent:

Total gross rent = $80 000

Annual outgoings : $7500

Purchase price : $1 000 000

(NIPA) = $80 000 − $7500 = $72 500

Net yield = ($72 500) / $1 000 000 × 100% = 7.25 per cent

If other properties are selling at yields of 7.25 per cent or lower, then you could have a very good deal on your hands.

To give you some basic philosophies about yield, let's talk about our three main commercial types: office, industrial and retail. Historically, industrial properties usually offer the best yield but have lower capital growth. In recent times, however, industrial properties have achieved the fastest growth due to an increase in demand as more businesses move online and the need for storage space grows.

In the office market, yields are lower than industrial in many areas. This is often due to higher quality finishes and higher per-square-metre values.

Finally, retail yields vary greatly. For example, a national supermarket might demand a sharp yield of 4 to 5 per cent net, but the hairdresser next door might be valued closer to a 7 per cent net yield. In general, the lower the yield the higher the calibre of tenant.

Historically, we've found yields are lower for retail versus industrial and office space in the areas we invest in. We attribute this to more people feeling comfortable with the idea of retail versus other types of assets, perhaps because people visit shops more than industrial properties. However, in recent times, post-COVID, people have become more fearful of retail and more comfortable with industrial. Retail growth has slowed as a result of greater competition from online businesses. But, as everywhere, we can expect swings and roundabouts in yields for each asset class. Please note that these comments are general in nature and exceptions won't be hard to find.

Yields are affected by the economy

In a strong economy yields can drop. Remember that when people are confident, they can more readily justify purchasing properties at sharper yields because they see more potential for growth. When confidence is high in an area or in the economy as a whole, people will pay more for assets. This means commercial property values can rise because investors are prepared to pay more for the same value of rent coming in annually. This causes yields to drop, which is commonly referred to as *yield compression*. When people ask us how commercial properties grow in value, we often refer to yield compression as a source of capital growth.

On the flip side, where the economy looks weaker and demand is lower, investors generally seek higher yields to justify their purchases. This is one of the reasons why you will see higher yields in the country areas versus capital cities — because investors need a higher yield to justify purchasing in a higher risk market.

So why are capital cities generally lower risk? Here's how it works. If you take a busy city like Sydney, it has plenty of businesses in operation and a pipeline of new ventures driven by a large population base. This depth in entrepreneurship provides more choice of future tenants, which lowers the vacancy risk for investors. The result of this lower risk is that higher prices will be paid, hence lower yields are expected for these types of areas. Conversely, smaller cities that show less demand can have longer vacancy periods simply because there are fewer tenants seeking to lease the average commercial property. Longer vacancies mean more risk, which leads to higher average market yields. However, don't make the mistake of automatically ruling out regional cities, as supply can sometimes be less, which can work in your favour on supply and demand ratios. It all comes down to local knowledge of the product, the demand, and the supply, and then factoring in the yield as a measure of the deal's quality.

As you can see, the local economy is a huge part of the equation, so never make the mistake of looking only for high yields. You need to have a balance of quality and a good yield to make a wise investment choice.

Yields are affected by a property's position

Put simply, the best locations tend to attract the best quality tenants. For example, KFC or McDonald's occupy some of the busiest retail precincts in every corner of the globe. If they were located in areas where there was no foot traffic or highway traffic, it would be harder for them to succeed.

As a commercial investor we want the best locations too. Investors will pay premiums for better locations due to the added security from having a better quality tenant occupy the property. The negative side of this is that paying this premium will lower your yield as the price you pay will be higher, as per the yield equation. Some will argue that this lower yield is worth it as there is more chance for capital growth with lower vacancy risk.

Yields are affected by interest rates

In recent times, interest rates have been getting lower and lower. And as the cost of borrowing gets cheaper, this helps investors pay more for properties. To explain, a few years ago interest rates were around 5–6 per cent in Australia. At the time, investors we worked with demanded 8 per cent net yields, which is roughly a 2–3 per cent buffer on the interest rates. In 2020, however, most investors are securing commercial loans around 3 per cent. So they don't need an 8 per cent yield to get a good return. Anything over 6 per cent net will give you that 3 per cent buffer. So interest rates have a direct influence on the yields you will see for commercial properties.

The right yield

Over the years we have finetuned plenty of techniques to build better passive income. We have found, for instance, that it's better to have a high-grade 6.5 per cent net yield in a capital city than a 10 per cent net yield in a small regional town. There are of course exceptions to this rule, but as a general guide, high yields can equal higher risk.

For example, if you bought a bank in a small town of fewer than 5000 people and the bank decided to vacate the premises, it might take years to replace the tenant. On the flip side, if you had a warehouse right next to an international airport, you might find it takes only a month or two to replace the tenant. Better quality properties in good areas lower the risk for the

Table 5: total 10-year rental income forecast

	Purchase price ($)	Yield (%)	Annual net rent ($)	Assumed vacancy (every 3 years)	Assumed rental growth (p.a.) (%)	Rent received over 10 years ($)
Capital city	700 000	6.50	45 500	2 months	3.5	506 758.53
Regional town	700 000	7.50	52 500	6 months	2	487 913.99

investor. We also see better rental growth over the long term for higher grade areas. This will mean your long-term yield will grow over time.

One thing we always do when assessing a property is map out a 10-year financial snapshot of the property. Table 5 compares a regional property with a high-grade one in a capital city.

The regional town property has a 7.5 per cent net yield versus 6.5 per cent in the capital city. Most people would assume the regional property would therefore offer a better cash flow. But this may be a false assumption when forecasting the total rental received over a 10-year period. This is because the rental growth will be better and the vacancy period will typically be shorter between each three-year lease for the property in the higher demand area. For this simple comparison we have assumed this higher demand area is the capital city example.

Once you factor in the shorter vacancies and the higher rent growth, you can see that the capital city property will collect $506758.53 in rent over 10 years, whereas in the same period of time the higher yielding regional property collects only $487913.99.

Let's be clear that regional properties can make fantastic investments. In fact, we help clients purchase regional properties every month. You just have to be careful not to become fixated on the initial yield. It's the yield after 10 years that is the big profit play for you as a long-term investor.

While we're on yields, you can't squeeze the yield too low as there will be a point where the cash flow is just not worth it. For example, we see some investors buying properties in Melbourne and Sydney at 1.5 to 3 per cent net yields. To us this is crazy because it defeats the purpose of choosing a commercial investment in the first place, which is to generate a passive income.

Remember, the goal is to create strong passive income for your retirement, not just to trap money in bricks and mortar and hope for growth.

HOW DO YOU MAKE MONEY OUT OF THIS?

There's little point investing in any property if you're not going to get a decent return. So let's dig a little deeper. In residential property, the value of a property is set by the market, and as we've described, these properties are bought differently and sold differently, based mainly on emotion and what price other houses of similar size have commanded.

Furthermore, residential properties are usually bought with a view to capital growth and building equity rather than annual cash flow profits, which means that as an investor you have less predictability over your investment returns. After all, capital growth is inherently difficult to predict at the best of times.

Commercial property is different. It often comes with long leases and typically has scheduled rental increases built into the lease. These factors are crucial. The scheduled rental increases are a key contributor when making money in commercial property. Because each year, the rental increase built into the contract, which you can negotiate as the owner of the property, gives you more cash to grow your income. So you'll know exactly how much rent you'll be receiving per annum in year one, two, three and so on. This makes it easier to bank on your cash flow returns, which should be significant when done right.

Connected with this is the way the value of a commercial property is calculated. In residential property, value is set by the market; in commercial property, value is directly proportionate to the income it generates.

You'll create capital growth/equity by adding in the annual rental increases to the lease, because the extra income raises the value of the asset. If you were to triple the rental income, you'd potentially triple the value.

This is why there's no emotion involved in commercial property investment, because it's purely a game of numbers. If you understand how to find properties that have a rental upside, you can create equity quickly by increasing the income. So maybe there is a little emotion after all!

Basically, the predictability of the lease and its inbuilt annual percentage increases actually helps you predict capital growth more confidently than with residential. And that's why we love it.

It's adopting these types of strategies that makes the game more interesting. Testing the many tools, tips and techniques for increasing rental income is among the most enjoyable aspects of commercial property investing. We'll dig into this in more detail later, but at this stage we just want you to get your head around the different mindset involved when dealing with commercial property. Add a few commercial properties to your portfolio and you will really start to see how you can build passive income into your lifestyle.

What is it going to cost?

Buying property of any kind can be pricey, and for some unattainable. Overvalued residential property markets can make investing prohibitive for some in the housing sector, where a 20 per cent deposit can set you back hundreds of thousands of dollars.

In the commercial market, you can start off with a deposit as low as $60 000. We recommend kicking off at $100 000, which would cover your deposit and purchase costs on a commercial property purchase of around $300 000. This is the price point we believe will provide the quality you need in an asset.

In many cases, if you already have built up some equity within an existing asset, such as your first house purchase, you can use that to secure your first commercial property investment.

So it's not as hard as you might think to get your foot on the ladder. Of course, a large retail space will have a larger price tag, but in this market there's plenty of diversity, so there's a wide mix of properties to choose from.

For example, buying a car park could cost you tens of thousands of dollars, rather than the hundreds of thousands you'd be expected to outlay in the residential sector. Investors are flocking out to look at small warehouses or 'man caves' as a good first investment. But we must stress that at these lower price points you should seek professional help to find the best quality possible, because the risk can be higher and the tenants may not stay as long as those for a larger property.

Whether you have a lot of capital to spend or a smaller amount to finance, commercial property will offer you amazing diversity. The hard part is to pick the best type of asset for your budget.

Why is commercial property so important for investors?

There are two main reasons:

- *High yields.* In an investment world where high yields are becoming increasingly difficult to find, commercial property offers investors a cash flow high enough to generate a significant passive income even after bank debt has been taken on. This places you in a much stronger position if you're planning for early retirement. And for us, that's the name of the game. Basically, commercial property can be a gold mine for investors looking to create a passive income for their retirement.

- *More flexible lending.* It's important to note that since the independent statutory authority APRA (Australian Prudential Regulation Authority) has made residential lending much more difficult, it's no longer as easy for investors to build large portfolios. This is because it's harder to meet the servicing requirements set by the banks. The more residential properties you buy, the harder it is to get another loan. Eventually, you will reach your lending limit — and it's game over for growing your portfolio. Fortunately, there is another way: commercial lending.

Yes, you heard that right. It is still possible to secure loans for commercial property even if you can no longer meet the residential serviceability requirements. Commercial loans are assessed differently and comprise 'lease doc loans', 'low doc loans' and 'no doc loans' that you can potentially take advantage of if you have run out of lending steam on the residential side. For more details on lease doc loans, please listen to the episode titled 'How to succeed in commercial property' from our podcast, *Inside Commercial Property by Rethink Investing*. In fact, hundreds of our commercial clients are investors with large residential portfolios who are now moving to commercial because it's where the lending is. More about strategic investing later.

Why are commercial investors important?

Businesses rely on investors to purchase their premises so they have the space they need to conduct their business. This is because most businesses won't have the capital to purchase their own commercial premises outright. If you think about it, it's no different from residential tenants needing landlords to provide them with housing because they haven't yet saved up a deposit for a house.

Additionally, commercial investors are good for the economy. Fewer investors underpinning commercial properties means fewer small businesses out there giving it a go. Many businesses rely on foot traffic and a high street presence, and an office is integral to their operation. They would face significant challenges if their only option was to buy their premises rather than renting it. So investors play a vital role in keeping the general economy in balance. Some jurisdictions have even waived stamp duty on commercial purchases to encourage investment. For example, in the ACT, no stamp duty is payable for commercial investments up to $1.5 million, and in South Australia, it has been completely abolished for commercial investments at any price point.

Why don't more commercial tenants purchase properties?

There is a huge owner-occupier market for commercial properties. This is because many owners purchase their office, shop or warehouse through their self-managed super fund (SMSF) or other structures to rent it back from themselves. Those who don't become owner-occupiers generally don't purchase for two main reasons:

1. They can't afford the outlay. The capital needed to purchase an entry-level commercial property must cover around 30 per cent with a loan on top and the ability to service that loan. For a small business, this is a lot of money.

2. Businesses often prioritise capital expenditure on business costs rather than on property costs. They see that this money is better spent on marketing, stock, staff and other costs, rather than hundreds of thousands or even millions spent on property. So many large businesses still choose to rent from investors, as they prefer to spend their money on growing the business rather than keeping it tied up in the real estate they occupy. It's a win/win between tenant and landlord.

BUSTING THE MYTHS

Like any investment, there are risks in chasing returns on commercial property. But from our experience, some of these commercial risks can be blown out of all proportion, most often exaggerated by individuals who have little to zero experience in the commercial asset class. It's probably not that different from other asset classes. For example, there are always crowds of people who are supremely confident that residential property is going to drop by 40 to 50 per cent, yet decade after decade that unlikely collapse never eventuates. Of course, the people who make these predictions are rarely property investors. That's why you need to know the facts, and hopefully why you're holding this book.

Before taking investment advice from someone, ask them if they own any commercial properties or have any direct experience with commercial property. Nine times out of ten, you'll find those warning you about various aspects of commercial property are not commercial investors themselves. Remember, residential investing is a very different game from commercial investing.

Commercial property triggers a fear of the unknown in many people. It's not as tangible as residential and harder to understand, which is why the myths are born.

So let's bust some of the biggest commercial myths out there.

Vacancies

This is probably the main reason people won't invest in commercial property. They assume you face a high risk of getting stuck with long vacancies, and they're concerned about the risk of the property standing empty for a long period of time. They see vacancy signs outside commercial buildings, sometimes for months, and assume that any commercial investment will likely suffer the same fate.

The truth is vacancies can be long for poor-quality assets but are generally shorter for high-grade, well-located properties. So investors need to carefully assess all relevant factors such as the quality of the building, the location, rent levels and the state of the general market around it. Getting the due diligence right will help ensure that the property won't stay vacant for long.

Never forget that properties in high-demand, low-supply areas will always be snapped up by tenants. If you purchase a commercial property in a poor location and the building is in disrepair, then of course the vacancy periods will be longer. It's all about buying good-quality properties with strong relettability potential.

Another point to make is that many leases have minimum vacate notice periods in the contract. These state that the tenant must give the landlord notice of anywhere between three to twelve months before leaving the property. If you are notified by your tenant six months out, then you have six months' rent coming in while you search for a new tenant. From our experience, tenants will often provide more than one year's notice because their business needs more time to plan and accomplish their relocation. As you can see, commercial leasing is very different from residential, where tenants can just pick up and leave with a day's notice.

To reiterate, if you know what you're doing and complete the proper due diligence ahead of time, you will have a much greater chance of reducing the risk of vacancy. The inevitability of long vacancies is a complete myth.

Only for the wealthy

This is another common myth we hear all the time. This is because people usually think of commercial property as commanding higher prices, which can be true, but there are thousands of exceptions to the rule.

Did you know that you can find commercial properties for as little as $250 000? In fact, we regularly secure commercial properties around this price for our clients and will continue to do so until prices rise. Obviously, as you move into the higher price brackets you will have a lot more assets to choose from.

Table 6 shows the amount of cash you would need for a $250 000 commercial purchase, assuming you could secure an 80 per cent commercial loan. As you can see, you would need only $63 400, which is within the reach of most first-time commercial investors.

Table 6: costings for a $250 000 commercial property

20% deposit	$50 000
Stamp duty	$7800
Building report	$600
Solicitor's fees	$3500
Strata report	$300
Bank valuation	$1200
Total	$63 400

We normally advise our clients to save upwards of $100 000 for a commercial investment, so they have a much wider selection to choose from. If you don't have this amount of money you'll get there simply by delaying the purchase for a little longer while you keep saving. We'll discuss this further in Part II.

Another alternative is to buy residential first, then move into commercial once you've built up sufficient equity. If you choose this path, you will first need to be confident of quick returns from residential property.

Low capital growth

We love breaking down this myth. So many people incorrectly assume that commercial properties are no good for capital growth. While some markets remain flat, we have seen commercial properties double or even triple in value over a 10-year period. So never assume commercial properties won't achieve strong capital growth. The question is how to improve your chances of buying a property that will get better growth than others? Let us explain.

As in the residential market, there are plenty of factors that can contribute to capital growth, including:

- good location
- scarcity factor
- infrastructure improvements
- population growth
- tightening vacancy rates
- strategic renovation potential
- loosening lending policies
- gentrification
- falling interest rates
- dropping unemployment figures.

Now guess what causes growth for commercial property?

All the above! Of course, there is no way to predict precisely the capital growth amount of any property, as these triggers all move independently. Some will impact more than others at certain points in the property cycle. Just remember that, as in the residential space, the commercial market responds to these economic improvements. The one big difference is that commercial property has more of its growth attached to its rental income. So increasing or improving the lease quality will have a larger overall impact on the commercial asset value. And just like any investment, if you choose the property carefully, you'll see growth.

Fewer value-add opportunities

We've also heard commercial naysayers argue that, unlike in the residential market, there are limited opportunities to create value-add opportunities. Sure, they say, you can attract incremental growth through inflation, but you'll gain nothing in the longer term from the property itself.

Well, we wouldn't be writing a book on commercial property if this were true. The fact is it's completely possible to raise long-lasting value on a commercial property if you know what to do. Unlike residential properties, where it's all about improving the liveability of a property, in commercial the numbers do all the talking.

As mentioned, much of the value of a commercial property is tied to its rental income, so finding properties that are under-rented can be the path to easy equity gains.

For example, a 500m^2 property renting for \$100 000 per annum is valued at \$200/m^2. If the market rent is \$240/m^2, the property is under-rented by 20 per cent. In that case, if you have a plan and the means to get the rent back up to market level, your income will be 20 per cent higher. And this could increase the value of the commercial property by 20 per cent, assuming you bought it at the correct yield from day one of course.

Another value add is strata titling or subdividing the property. This adds value because you can sell or rent smaller sections at a higher per-square-metre rate. For example, a 1000m^2 warehouse might rent for \$100/m^2. But five 200m^2 warehouses could potentially rent at \$130/m^2. Essentially, you are reversing the 'economies of scale' in your favour, and your value could increase by 30 per cent due to the higher rent per square metre.

There are other value-adds too, including renovating, lengthening leases, rezoning and developing. Just as with residential property, there are many opportunities to add value. You just have to be aware of the fundamental principles in play.

PART I SUMMARY

Once you have reviewed our first commercial property purchase experience and explored the fundamentals of the commercial property market as outlined in Part I, you'll start to connect the dots between theory and practice.

And that's exactly what it takes—practice. During our first few property purchases, we began to clock up thousands of hours researching and investigating potential property deals. We were starting to build some real intelligence around what it takes to become successful in this game.

As you now know, there are many property types, each of them with their own levers. It can be hard to know what to buy and when, but once you get your head around the two key elements of commercial property—cash flow positive and yields—you'll be streets ahead.

We've busted some of the common myths. We've heard them so many times, but it's only when you confront and get past these fallacies that you can start to see beyond your backyard and appreciate why we love investing in commercial property to build our wealth.

To make money, you'll need to aim for high-grade but also high-yielding commercial deals. But outside the numbers and details of the commercial properties themselves is another, perhaps even more important element you need to bring to the table—the right mindset. We'll discuss this further in Part II.

You're now ready to move from theory to practice through our practical '7 Steps' program. This will give you the 'how' when purchasing property, while also demonstrating how we ourselves work.

PART II
THE 7 STEPS

In Part I we explored the theory and the 'what' of commercial property. We explained the ins and outs of the commercial property industry and shared with you our own personal journey of how we climbed that first rung of the commercial ladder, along with many lessons we've learned over the past decade. It wasn't always easy, and looking back now we cringe when we recall some of the things we did—or didn't do.

Now it's time to learn the practice of how to go about it. When we began building our portfolio, we soon discovered how some of the things we were doing were needlessly repetitive, following a similar path regardless of the property. We saw where our processes were duplicated and began to develop ways to systematise our approach. The more we invested, the more familiar we became with tools and techniques we could use to build our portfolio faster. This helped us finetune our approach.

We found ourselves following a consistent pathway for every prospective property we became interested in, and subsequently when we bought it, which made our work easier and helped us determine whether the property suited our needs. Over time, we turned that pathway into a series of standardised steps and a clear process to help us buy properties faster once we were persuaded that the numbers made sense. Before long our seven steps became a crucial tool, and we began to use it with our clients too.

So, without further ado, here are the '7 Steps' that we guarantee will help you become a successful commercial property investor:

1. **Money habits**. How much is enough? This is still one of the commonest questions we're asked about property. It's a question that's fundamental to setting your path to success. For your initial deposit, we believe a good starting point is $50 000 for residential property and $100 000 for commercial. These amounts are based on an entry-level $300 000 purchase price for both types of investment, though obviously the larger the deposit you can save, the more options you will have.

2. **Investment mindset**. It's hard to do anything well without the right mindset. The importance of entering into any activity with the right mindset is written about endlessly, and for good reason. Who you are as a person will influence the way you invest. Without a strong mindset, you're going to struggle to see anything beyond your backyard. With the right mindset, you can better set goals that suit you. We are big goal setters at Rethink. It's about setting the right priorities to get you where you want to be, and about setting your expectations around what you will experience when becoming a long-term commercial property owner.

3. **Asset selection**. There are many ways to find the right property. In the commercial property world, you need to arm yourself with the right information to uncover the gold. By understanding the growth drivers and other factors that influence the economy as a whole, you'll put yourself in the best position to secure the best property for your portfolio and goals.

4. **Method of sale**. Once you've selected the right asset, it's time to get to grips with the different ways to buy it. We recommend securing a property with a contract subject to finance approval and sufficient time for due diligence. This method provides the buyer with the greatest protection. It's not the only option, though, and each has its own set of rules, all of which must be fully understood.

5. **Finance**. How are you going to pay for your investment property? You'll need a bank loan, and it will require some effort on your part to come up with the information to secure the money. Luckily, you have a bunch of other financing instruments at your disposal to help you grow a larger commercial property portfolio and secure a better return on your equity.

6. **The negotiations**. Not all deals are created equal. As you're the one holding the cards it's up to you to get the deal done, so you need to be prepared to flex your negotiating muscles. Negotiations

aren't war, though; they are simply pathways to a final agreement. You need to do your homework and take out all the emotion so often associated with purchasing a residential property. If you work with the sellers, they will work with you. Negotiations are all about creating a win/win solution for both parties.

7. **Managing the property and understanding the tax**. Will you manage it yourself or employ a property manager? Whether you own the property through a company, a self-managed super fund (SMSF) or a discretionary trust, or as an individual, there are specific tax benefits that you need to be aware of. Get the ownership structure right, and you'll become an expert in capital gains tax, GST and negative gearing.

Let's kick things off by focusing on your money habits.

MONEY HABITS

Before you can become an investor, you must be a good saver, because without savings it's almost impossible to do anything in property. (There are some rare exceptions to this, such as vendor finance and property options, but these are unlikely scenarios for high-demand assets, as vendors will always prefer to sell in the traditional way if they can.)

Saving for a cash deposit is the number one barrier for many people seeking to get into the market. In Australia, the problem is exacerbated by the high price of housing. In many parts of the country it costs 10 times the average income to buy a mid-priced house. So getting into good savings habits early on in life will give you a major advantage.

Typically, the minimum cash deposit for residential real estate in Australia is 10 per cent of the purchase price. However, many people wait until they have saved 20 per cent to avoid having to pay lenders' mortgage insurance (LMI) on top of the loan.

There are also other costs such as stamp duty, solicitor costs and building/pest reports, and it's always wise to have a contingency/buffer in place when buying a property. We'll talk more about this in the next step.

For now, table 7 (overleaf) shows the purchasing costs based on the national average house price in Australia in March 2020—$611063, according to the ABS.

As this table shows, you will need to save about $143400 to buy an average house in Australia. Given the average Australian annual income of $86252, it can take a number of years for many income earners to break into the housing market. Luckily there are some shortcuts, which we'll explore later in the chapter.

Table 7: purchasing costs based on $554 000 house

House price	$611 063
Deposit (20%)	122 212
Stamp duty	23 000
Conveyancing	2000
Building/pest inspections	600
Contingency costs/buffer	10 000
Total	$157 812

Savings strategies

Before we continue, let's look at Mina's tips on saving, which helped us into our first property in Sutherland. It's worth noting that these tips are not for everyone, but they worked for us and we think they're worth sharing:

- *Set a savings goal.* Set yourself a fixed-amount target—a $100 000 deposit is our recommendation for commercial property. This will give you something to work towards. You can break it down into smaller, more achievable increments. For example, if you want to save $100 000 over three years, your goal is to put away $641 a week.

- *Save a percentage of your income.* If a large-figure goal like this doesn't work for you, think about saving a certain percentage of your income. This percentage will vary, depending on your living expenses. For example, if you earn $1000 per week, aim to put away 20 per cent of your income or $200 per week. This amount will grow as your income grows. You could also open a savings account once you have your goals worked out. Use a dedicated online savings account to store and manage your money. Unlike with a transaction account, you can't spend money directly from a savings account so it's harder to dip into your savings. To grow your savings faster, look for an account with a high interest rate and no fees.

- *Reduce unnecessary costs.* It's important to control your impulse spending. Focus on reducing recurring expenses as much as possible. Try to master the 30-day rule. Waiting 30 days to decide on a purchase is an excellent way to give you a better perspective on whether you truly need it.

- *Be patient.* It's important to recognise that you're going to need to be disciplined for a long period of time to save the equivalent of a deposit for a house. All too often people give up after six months and spend up big on a holiday because their friends are going overseas. Remember, you don't need to 'keep up with the Joneses'! You are denying yourself instant gratification for a more important long-term goal—a bigger long-term payoff for your future.

- *Pick jobs that pay well.* This might not be possible for everyone, depending on your qualifications or skill sets, but it's worth a mention. Picking a job that pays well may sound obvious, but some people choose jobs based solely on lifestyle or enjoyment. We see so many talented young people with a university education pursuing careers where their prospects and pay are below expectations. Scott would have preferred to be a ski instructor in Europe when he was 20, but he chose instead to become an engineer. Why? Because it was one of the best paying graduate roles out there.

- *Work hard from a young age.* Obviously, most people who read this book will have been working for many years, but this is a good lesson to teach your kids. As we outlined in the introduction, we both worked while still at school and had many jobs before turning 20. Not only did these jobs give us a small savings base, but they also helped us to secure better paying jobs as adults. Scott remembers his engineering boss once saying, 'I don't really care about the school/university you went to. I liked the fact you worked at McDonald's.' So working from a young age can accelerate your job prospects and eventually help you save faster.

So how did we save for our first deposits? We worked many jobs from a young age. Mina put every dollar she could into a savings account and never touched the money other than in an emergency. Scott disliked his engineering job, but it paid comparably well and set him up in his property career. Back then it was the only thing that got him through what felt like the wrong career choice, because he knew that something better was up ahead. So he used his salary to save as much as he could. More importantly, it helped him save quickly, which in turn enabled him to buy more properties at such a young age.

CASE STUDY
A residential property

To explain these numbers in more detail, first let's break down the costs of purchasing a $332 500 residential purchase (summarised in table 8):
- A 10 per cent deposit is based on a typically high lending ratio of 90 per cent for a residential loan.

- Note that LMI (lenders' mortgage insurance) will be added on to your loan for any loan over 80 per cent.

- Stamp duty costs will vary between states.

- We have allowed for a buffer of $5000.

Table 8: purchasing costs based on a $332 500 house

House price	$332 500
10% deposit (minimum)	$33 250
Stamp duty	$11 044
Conveyancing	2000
Building/pest inspections	600
Contingency costs/buffer	5000
Total	$51 894

Here's an example from our own experience. We purchased this property for a client in Brisbane in February 2020 for $332 500.

Details:
- Low-set brick home on a 650m². block
- 30-minute drive to Brisbane CBD and 45-minute drive to the Gold Coast
- Impressive gross yield of 5.78 per cent
- Rental appraisal at $370 per week

Now let's look at our cash flow. Table 9 (overleaf) shows the cash flow based on many different interest rate percentages and loan ratios. We also look at the impact the outgoings have on the cash flow. Residential purchases include the costs of council rates, insurance, rental management, plus landlord insurance and interest costs. Units and townhouses may have other costs such as body corporate/sinking fund expenses.

Table 9: rental potential at $360 per week

Price	$332 500
Rent	$360
Depreciation	$1500
Capital gains	5%
Rental mgt	7%

Property type	House
Building insurance	700
Landlord insurance	300
Rates + water (approx..)	3420
Repairs	1500

	Purchase price ($)	Annual rent ($)	Depreciation benefit ($)	Capital gains ($)	Interest ($)	Rent mgt ($)	Repairs	Insurance, water bills. land rates etc.	Cash return
Cash buy ($)	$332 500	$18 720	$1500	$16 625	$0	$1310	$0	$5920	$12 990
80 loan @4.25%	$332 500	$18 720	$1500	$16 625	$11 305	$1310	$0	$5920	$1685
90 loan @4.25%	$332 500	$18 720	$1500	$16 625	$12 718	$1310	$0	$5920	$271
100 loan @4.25%	$332 500	$18 720	$1500	$16 625	$14 131	$1310	$0	$5920	-$1142
105 loan @ 4.25%	$332 500	$18 720	$1500	$16 625	$14 838	$1310	$0	$5920	-$1848
80 loan at 4.5%	$332 500	$18 720	$1500	$16 625	$11 970	$1310	$0	$5920	$1020
90 loan at 4.5%	$332 500	$18 720	$1500	$16 625	$13 466	$1310	$0	$5920	-$477
100 loan at 4.5%	$332 500	$18 720	$1500	$16 625	$14 963	$1310	$0	$5920	-$1973
105 loan @ 4.5%	$332 500	$18 720	$1500	$16 625	$15 711	$1310	$0	$5920	-$2721
80 loan @ 4.75%	$332 500	$18 720	$1500	$16 625	$12 635	$1310	$0	$5920	$355
90 loan @ 4.75%	$332 500	$18 720	$1500	$16 625	$14 214	$1310	$0	$5920	-$1225
100 loan @ 4.75%	$332 500	$18 720	$1500	$16 625	$15 794	$1310	$0	$5920	-$2804
105 loan @ 4.75%	$332 500	$18 720	$1500	$16 625	$16 583	$1310	$0	$5920	-$3594
80 loan @ 5%	$332 500	$18 720	$1500	$16 625	$13 300	$1310	$0	$5920	-$310
90 loan @ 5%	$332 500	$18 720	$1500	$16 625	$14 963	$1310	$0	$5920	-$1973
100 loan @ 5%	$332 500	$18 720	$1500	$16 625	$16 625	$1310	$0	$5920	-$3635
105 loan @ 5%	$332 500	$18 720	$1500	$16 625	$17 456	$1310	$0	$5920	-$4467

CASE STUDY

A commercial property

Now let's look at a similar priced commercial property by comparison. As we've outlined, the deposit tends to be larger in commercial transactions. Commercial property generally needs a deposit of 20 to 35 per cent, depending on the type of property you are buying (among other factors).

Table 10 shows the total numbers for a 75 per cent loan-to-value ratio (LVR) on a $308 000 commercial purchase:

- 25 per cent deposit

- 75 per cent LVR

- Stamp duty costs will vary between states

- You will see that we have allowed a buffer of $10 000, twice that for the residential property, to cover the worst-case possibility of longer vacancies.

Table 10: costings for a 75% LVR on a $308 000 commercial purchase

Commercial property price	**$308 000**
25% deposit	77 000
Stamp duty	10 000
Conveyancing	2000
Building/pest inspections	600
Contingency costs/buffer	10 000
Total	**$99 600**

Here's an example of a recent commercial property we helped one of our clients to purchase (see table 11, overleaf).

Details:
- Style: industrial warehouse

- Location: Brisbane

- Price paid: $308 000

- Rental income: $22 464 pa + tenant pays 100 per cent of outgoings

- Lease: 3 years + 3-year option

- Rental increase pa: 4 per cent

- Other: purchased off market roughly $35 000 below the market value of others selling in the same complex.

Now, if you compare the figures in our commercial cash flow table, you can see that the numbers stack up much more favourably for the similar-priced property.

On an 80 per cent loan, the residential property in the first example is going to give you an income of $1685 per annum. That's pretty good, considering most other residential properties would be lucky to break even, especially if there are strata costs or larger maintenance bills.

However, this is a small return compared to the commercial investment cash flow. For the same value and loan ratio, the commercial property will produce an annual passive income of roughly $18 724. Which is considerably better cash flow! And there are other benefits – for example, the tenant pays 100 per cent of the outgoings. This means no nasty unanticipated maintenance bills (not that much would ever go wrong with a concrete built warehouse) and a comfortable three-year lease.

Purchasing a property of this value to clear $18 724 per annum is not a bad start for your retirement. The trick is to keep building on it. To give you an idea, most of our clients set a goal to purchase up to ten of these in their lifetime. This would essentially create a $180 000 passive income that's growing every year. Not a bad way to invest!

Table 11: Commercial rental potential

Price	$308000	
Rent	$22464	(net of outgoings)
Depreciation	$5000	

Rental mgt	6 per cent

	Purchase price	Annual rent	Depreciation benefit	Interest	Rent mgt	Cash return
Cash buy	$308000	$22464	$5000	$0	$1348	$26116
70 loan @ 3%	$308000	$22464	$5000	$6468	$1348	$19648
75 loan @ 3%	$308000	$22464	$5000	$6930	$1348	$19186
80 loan @ 3%	$308000	$22464	$5000	$7392	$1348	$18724
100 loan @ 3%	$308000	$22464	$5000	$9240	$1348	$16876
70 loan @ 3.5%	$308000	$22464	$5000	$7546	$1348	$18570
75 loan @ 3.5%	$308000	$22464	$5000	$8085	$1348	$18031
80 loan @ 3.5%	$308000	$22464	$5000	$8624	$1348	$17492
100 loan @ 3.5%	$308000	$22464	$5000	$10780	$1348	$15336
70 loan @ 4%	$308000	$22464	$5000	$8624	$1348	$17492
75 loan @ 4%	$308000	$22464	$5000	$9240	$1348	$16876
80 loan @ 4%	$308000	$22464	$5000	$9856	$1348	$16260
100 loan @ 4%	$308000	$22464	$5000	$12320	$1348	$13796
70 loan @ 5%	$308000	$22464	$5000	$10780	$1348	$15336
75 loan @ 5%	$308000	$22464	$5000	$11550	$1348	$14566
80 loan @ 5%	$308000	$22464	$5000	$12320	$1348	$13796
100 loan @ 5%	$308000	$22464	$5000	$15400	$1348	$10716

What can we learn from this?

You need more savings to successfully invest in commercial property because of the lower lending ratios offered by commercial loans. Remember, though, that most residential investors wouldn't want a 90 per cent loan on a property just to avoid the LMI costs. So if you factor that in, the required savings amounts are almost the same for commercial versus residential.

Something else to consider is that, like many looking to move into commercial investing, you probably already own a property—your own home—and you can use the equity in your home as a springboard into investment property at sometimes much higher price points. In fact, about half our clients are homeowners using equity out of their principal place of residence. Depending on their equity levels, they can consider commercial properties at much higher price points. Just one or two such purchases can create significant passive incomes, essentially fast-tracking their retirement.

Here are a few other tips and tricks you have up your sleeve if you want to buy while putting less money down:

- *Using a higher LVR.* It is possible to borrow up to 95 per cent of a property's value. But it does trigger extra LMI costs, so you need to be careful. Generally, the higher the lending ratio the greater the perceived risk. The cash flow from your property will be weaker due to the extra repayments you must make to the bank to cover the higher interest costs. The 95 per cent loans are not available in commercial lending, but as mentioned it is possible to borrow 100 per cent of the property's value if you are drawing the deposit and subsequent loan from another asset, such as your home equity.

- *Joint ventures (JV).* You may consider attracting a partner to sponsor the upfront costs of the purchase, then splitting the proceeds. Most important in any JV is total trust between partners. You also need to make sure all partners are on the same page. Of course, the catch is you'll end up with only half the proceeds of the deal. There are two types of partners in a typical JV—equity partners and finance partners. Equity partners pay the deposit and buying costs, while the finance partner gets the loan from the bank.

- *Buying off-the-plan.* You may choose to buy a property before it's built and, provided it increases in value by the time it is constructed, you can borrow against the new value to fund your deposit. However, buying property off-the-plan is highly risky, so be careful. Yes, it can be a clever way to purchase with little funding, but it only works when purchased at a good price and in a growing market. The development also needs to have a long lead time.

- *Option agreements.* This one isn't so great for first home buyers, as it involves a higher level of skill and sophistication. The idea is to find a vendor who will agree to an option agreement by which you have the right—but not the obligation—to buy their property. The aim of many option agreements is to push settlement long into the future. As the potential buyer, you will look for ways to increase the value of the property and on-sell it for a profit. But it's not easy. Not many vendors are willing to enter into this type of arrangement, in which they must be prepared to delay settlement, sometimes by years, while you enjoy the capital growth and benefits, and whatever value you can add to it. Such agreements are more common in weak markets with distressed sellers.

YOUR TAKEAWAYS

More savings directly impacts our next step – mindset – because without the safety net of our savings, we would have been less likely to take the risks we did. We found comfort in the knowledge that if we stuffed up a deal, or got something wrong, we had our savings to fall back on. We could still meet our everyday expenses; we could pick ourselves up and look to reinvesting without compromising our current standard of living too dramatically.

From a savings perspective, this mindset certainly helped to give us the space to think outside our backyard and do things differently.

INVESTMENT MINDSET

It's hard to make much investment progress these days without the right mindset. A really important part of this is understanding who you are as a person, because this will ultimately impact the way you invest.

As we've stressed, this book isn't about knuckling down and saving for a home and being 'comfortable'. It's about making your money work for you as effectively as possible, taking risks and getting *uncomfortable*, which can lead you to take the plunge and buy your dream home, or to pursue your investment goals in a bold but informed way.

Our own goals as property investors were never complicated and could be summed up as:

- simply being happy
- spending more time with family
- travelling overseas as often as we like
- living comfortably in a home we love
- having the flexibility to work when and where we want.

Whether investing in commercial or residential properties, keeping these goals front and centre has ensured that we remain focused and on track.

We switched to commercial property investing because we wanted to diversify our portfolio by putting some of our eggs in a different basket, instead of focusing purely on residential properties. We were also looking for new challenges by pushing the boundaries. Residential is a safe way to get into investing, but we found there were more pros than cons to investing in commercial property.

We were first attracted to commercial investing for the following main reasons:

- The tenancy agreements are most often three to five years, where residential terms are generally three, six or twelve months.

- Business owners are generally easier to deal with than residential tenants.

- All outgoings are paid by the tenant.

Confident of these benefits, we anticipated 'easier management with fewer touch points'. This was important because at the time we were working very hard keeping on top of our residential properties. And the bigger our portfolio grew, the more we seemed to be moving away from the goal of 'buying back our time'.

Moving to commercial early on was a hard switch, as we had nowhere near as much knowledge of the topic. But as an asset class, it felt so much more in tune with our goals of getting better results from high-quality properties with business tenants. Looking back at this moment shows us it was one of the best moves we ever made with investing.

There were no shortcuts to our success in this asset class. We learned simply by putting thousands of hours into searching, teaching ourselves, and eventually buying and managing our investments ourselves.

The fear mindset

Once you know what drives you, you will be able to make decisions with the right mindset. Because, as already noted, being in the right mindset when approaching property, whether it's commercial or residential, is the key to good investing.

When it comes to choosing between residential and commercial property, a lot of people *fear* what they don't know. People know more about residential property, less about commercial investing. Fear blocks us from doing many things. For evidence of that you need look no further than the sheer number of investors in residential as opposed to commercial. Relatively, there aren't that many in our neck of the woods!

If you're really determined to achieve your goals, which we're guessing is why you picked up this book, you must get past the fear of exploring the unknown.

Opportunistic mindset

As we've mentioned, this type of investing is for those who don't want to sit on their negative or neutrally geared assets while hoping for growth over the long term. For us that model was too slow, and it was never going to produce a worthwhile passive income for our retirement either.

We're guessing you're reading this book because you are the type of investor who wants to speed up results and you're not afraid of plunging into something new to do so.

When it comes to property, it's important to see beyond what everyone else sees. We're not here to purchase the 'prettiest' property to make us feel happy and nice. We're here to make money from our investments. We need to see past the 'dirt', such as décor, to ask:

- Does this property cover all the bases we have identified?
- Will finance options be favourable for this asset?
- Will the rent cover our mortgage, rates and other expenses?
- Does it represent a good yield?
- Is it in a location that is developing and growing?
- Does it tick all the boxes on our due diligence check list?
- Is there an opportunity to add value (in the short or long term)?
- If a tenant leaves, how long would it take to find a new one?

If you can look past what others see as flaws in a property and value the costs of their remediation in your own mind, you can purchase better based on the numbers compared to your everyday investor.

Rolling with the punches mindset

Another point to consider is how you handle it when things turn sour. Because let's be honest, over time you will have to deal with problems, such as losing a tenant at a bad time or copping a large unanticipated maintenance bill. These issues are part of property ownership and you must have a plan of how to handle them.

Vacancies can be challenging, but you have to stay positive and work out solutions. Remind yourself, 'Well hang on, I've made my money back already via growth,' or why not take advantage of the vacancy by doing minor fix-ups and renting it for more?

In other words, you need to be able to roll with the punches. Property can generate amazing long-term wealth, but some people expect results without hiccups. Investors must be ready for some adverse events or they can become pretty discouraged. You need to be prepared for:

- unexpected maintenance bills
- tenants trashing your property
- long vacancies
- market downturns
- poor rental managers
- complaints from tenants or neighbours
- your property being robbed.

Some of these events can come as a big shock if you're new to investing. But we've developed a trick over the years to help put things in perspective. It involves looking at the total return on investment, which helps put the day-to-day problems in context:

- Work out the cost of the issue. For example, if the air conditioner blew up and needs replacing, it might cost you $2000.

- Work out how much money you could make from the investment over a 10-year period. For example, a $500 000 property with

6 per cent growth per annum for 10 years will make about $345 000. Adopt a different perspective, and suddenly that $2000 seems inconsequential (especially when you can claim it as a tax deduction).

- When you have a bad day with maintenance or vacancy, remember you're playing the long game. You will make money out of this investment, but you need to look beyond the day-to-day issues that can stress you out.

If you have the mindset that recognises sometimes things go wrong, and that you just have to roll with the punches without the punches getting the better of you, then congratulations, you're already a true investor! Part of the mindset is recognising the importance of removing all emotion when investing in the commercial market. You must have the stamina and the stomach to be an investor, because it is a never-ending rollercoaster with new surprises around every corner.

And—surprise! Not everyone is cut out for it. For some, fear or frustration overwhelms them, and that's understandable. When we invest, we take the plunge only once we're satisfied with all our calculations. We do our research and our checks to ensure we enter into the negotiations with a clear mind, knowing it's the right choice. We know that with any property there will be highs and lows, and we ride the wave. And we encourage all our clients to adopt a similar mindset.

Profit mindset – short and long term

Time and time again, we've found that the surest path to success is to plan to make money in both the short and the long term. It sounds incredibly basic, but I promise you a large percentage of novice investors don't think about exactly how they can profit at both levels. They buy for different reasons—having 'a good feeling' about the area or because the house presents well, or for some other arbitrary reason. Rather than relying on such loose thinking we recommend you follow our tried and tested procedure on profit goal setting—a three-year view for profit and a 10-year-plus view for long-term wealth.

Three-year view for profit

When we invest in property, it's for the long term. However, we also plan to profit in the short term in what we call the three-year window from purchase.

There are many ways to do this, but as a start we look to profit via cash flow. Take this recent example of a commercial property we helped one of our clients purchase in Queensland:

- Purchase price: $890 000 (net yield: 7.8 per cent).

- Cost to hold: 70 per cent finance is being used ($890 000 × 70 per cent = $623 000), at 3.5 per cent interest ($21 805 per annum).

- Cashflow profit: Net income is $69 046 per annum, with the cost to hold at $47 241 per annum (or $908 per week)

- Factoring in captial growth, this $890 000 purchase will make the client approximately $150 000 in just a three year period.

Comparing apples with apples, imagine you purchase a house or unit for the same money at a cost of $15 000 per annum to hold (this is a typical Sydney or Melbourne residential unit), that would mean there is a $45 000 negative cash flow position in just three years, putting the two assets almost $200 000 apart in a cash flow profit sense. So unless the residential property grows by more than $200 000 in just three years and the commercial property doesn't grow at all, then the commercial investment will bring greater profits. Let this sink in and you will start to see how you can make considerably more money out of commercial investing.

Many investors who negatively gear look only for a tax benefit in the short term, while hoping the property will grow in the long run. This lowers their chances of making a short-term profit because the returns are much reduced once they take account of their negative cash flow. Or they might overpay for a property just to get into the market.

So how can you plan to make money by adopting the three-year view for profit? You may purchase a property under market value, achieve exceptional cash flow or purchase into a market that is rising in value quickly. In each case, your goal is to make money in the short term. And all three of these methods can be applied to commercial property.

10-year-plus view for long-term wealth

On the other hand, some investors concentrate only on short-term results. But this can impact their long-term investment return results. It can be a mistake, for example, to buy a property with the goal of flipping it for a quick profit, especially when you take into account the major costs of buying the property (stamp duty) and of selling it (sales agent fees plus capital gains tax). You might also end up selling too early. Smart investors in Australia look to hold their investments for at least 10 years, because in a country with an economic track record as strong as Australia's, it makes sense to hold property for the long term.

It's also important to purchase in a market with a good long-term growth forecast. For example, we've never been fans of mining towns or other markets that can quickly go from boom to bust. These types of markets are too difficult to predict over a 10-year-plus period. Regional properties are fine, but you want to see a consistent pattern of population growth to feel confident in the 10-year investment window.

Adopting a 10-year-plus view for long-term wealth could include purchasing quality assets in built-out capital city suburbs where supply is limited and tenant demand is high. Or purchasing a property with a good-quality land component, because this land will appreciate over time and may lead to long-term development upsides. Again, all these elements can be found in commercial property, with the bonus of high cash flow, which makes holding such investments for long periods a whole lot more fun.

Be sure not to chase all-out yield and neglect the fundamentals. As illustrated in table 5 (see page 27), having an initial higher yield in a lower growth market can actually result in less cash-flow over a 10-year period. It's important to have a good yield but also strong capital growth prospects.

Your mindset

Let's turn this over to you. Sometimes it's tricky to work out what you want, so here are a few ideas to help you think about what drives you, what your goals are and what you need to do to get there. Then tackle it head on. We've learned over time that the only thing holding you back is you. And you can decide to propel yourself forward. Ask yourself:

- What makes you happy?
- Have you achieved it?
- If not, what's holding you back?
- Do you really want to do this?
- Do you deserve this? Why?
- What hurdles do you need to overcome?

With a little more insight, you can now turn your attention to your property goals, and how you can achieve your higher goals through the property market.

First you need to get your priorities in order. We believe that investment-related goals should be centred on annual passive income amounts. For example, if you believe you need $150 000 passive income to live a comfortable life in retirement, that figure should be the goal you drive towards.

Having an income goal to aim for will change the way you invest. You won't be looking for risky short-term investments; instead, you'll look to invest in higher yielding properties, which will promote the idea of saving money.

We create three-year plans then break them down into $50 000 increments. For example, a person saving $40 000 per annum with a $120 000 current cash deposit may have as a goal to reach $50 000 annual passive income in three years' time, with capital growth on top.

Building a successful property portfolio is like building a business. You need to focus on growth and revenue.

Assembling your expert team

Do you think of property investing as something you can handle yourself, or as better left to professionals? We think of it as a trade. Ask yourself this: Would you go and perform brain surgery because you think you could do it yourself? Or would you entrust it to someone who has many years of training and experience in the field? Of course, brain surgery is an extreme case, but isn't it the same for a tiler or plumber or even a web designer and coder? You turn to someone who knows their stuff really well. Sometimes, even if you are a highly experienced investor, consulting an expert will bring a new dimension to your decision making.

There's sure to be factors you'll miss if you try to invest in a new asset class yourself, because there are a lot of moving parts. For example, working in various states can be tricky, and you need to find experts who understand the different legal jurisdictions, because cooling-off periods and other regulations can vary from state to state.

On the other hand, a professional who understands the complexities of investing inside out can do the groundwork for you. You're paying for their expertise and experience. We seek advice only from people who know more than us and have already achieved what we want to achieve.

Finding your expert team requires lots of research. Use your professional networks and word of mouth. It may be a bit hit and miss, as we have experienced over the years, but the more exposure you open yourself up to, and the more you are willing to get involved in the industry, the more people you will meet. But you must be willing to dedicate time to start building your network.

Your team members must be organised and pay attention to detail. They need to act fast and never delay a process. A property sale doesn't wait around for someone to finish their dinner! You have to move fast. The right team understands that the process of investing (the way we do it) is critical to our success. Surrounding yourself with experienced players who understand the investing *process* and the reasons *why* you are investing is also a must.

Let's meet the most important people on your team.

Mortgage broker

A broker understands the lending process and how to maximise your borrowing capacity as your portfolio grows. They shop around many providers in order to offer you:

- the best deal with the lowest fees on accounts
- the lowest interest rate
- the longest loan terms to help extend your serviceability
- sound advice on what will best fit your borrowing needs.

Brokers are paid by the banks when you settle successfully. If you stay with that bank, they also receive a trailing commission over time, so it's important to choose a broker you trust. Many will keep you with the same bank, even if there are better deals out there, because it saves them time—and they can get extremely busy. So it's very important to have a good relationship with your broker, which means you can call them up and have them regularly review your loans. Shopping around every 12 or 24 months will often pay off in gaining you a better deal on your loans. Brokers who are keepers do what is needed to accommodate all the changes required to refinance with the banks, even if it means losing their commission.

Buyer's agent

A buyer's agent can make the biggest difference as they can deliver investment-grade properties you would have never before seen or considered. If they are not sufficiently experienced, though, they can also get it horribly wrong. A good buyer's agent knows and understands the market in depth and will deploy this understanding on your behalf. With many years of investment experience across multiple property cycles, a good agent can guide you towards the outcomes they have achieved for themselves. It is therefore vital to choose an agent who is already in a position you aspire to be in.

It's also important that they have invested in recent times and know how to make money in the current market. There's no point in working with an agent whose strategies aren't aligned with your appetite for risk or who promotes dated strategies that worked 20 years ago. Your buyer's agent will provide you with strategic advice and source the properties for you. You'll also entrust them with the decision to say no to properties if they consider them a bad choice.

Your broker and buyer's agent must work well together so everyone is on the same page. Many times we've been rattled when the brokers and agents (ourselves) have come to different conclusions, creating confusion all round.

If you expand your portfolio in the future with a mix of commercial and residential properties, you'll need to ensure that your team understands how both markets work. Brokers can re-evaluate your situation and refinance when needed. We refinance every couple of years, using brokers who are themselves also property investors.

The cost of using a buyer's agent ranges widely. Generally, they are paid at settlement (although companies vary and some expect to be paid before settlement). The price will depend on the property bought. Some are fixed and others are based on a percentage. Some charge a sign-up fee and some expect one lump sum. Sign-up fees can range from $1000 to $5000, and the commission can range from $9000 to $15 000. For larger value purchases, percentage charges are more common than fixed amounts. A percentage rate can range between 1.5 and 3.5 per cent.

Property manager

Once you've reached settlement, you need to make sure you have a good property manager who understands that this is an *investment*, so doesn't waste money on things that don't align with the bigger picture. There's nothing worse than a neglectful agent who fails to do the right thing, especially when the investment is in a different state from where you live.

Property managers take a monthly commission according to the number of tenancies they manage. The rates vary between different cities. Table 12 (overleaf) gives you a rough idea of the different fees for rental management that apply in each state.

Table 12: rental management fee comparisons

	Residential (%)	Commercial* (%)
Sydney	4–6	3–5.5
Melbourne	5–7	4–6
Brisbane	7–8.8	4–6
Perth	7–10	5–8
Canberra	6–8	4–6
Adelaide	7–9	5–7
Hobart	7–11	5–8
Darwin	6–9	5–8

* Depending on your lease agreement, you may be able to on-charge the cost of rental management back to the commercial tenant.

Accountant

Before making an offer to buy a property, obtain advice from a property tax expert (such as an accountant) about the best structure to use for your offer.

The popular tax structures available for property investors are:

- individually in your name
- jointly with a partner or spouse
- joint venture (JV)
- family discretionary trust
- unit trust
- self-managed super fund (SMSF).

Most people have their own trusted accountant they've used for years, but it's important to use an accountant who is an expert in property tax. If you use a non-specialist, you may end up purchasing the property under the wrong structure, which could cost you tens or even hundreds of thousands of dollars in the long run.

All the above structures have different tax implications that must be properly taken account of. Only an accountant who understands your long-term property investment strategy will be able to provide the best advice for you.

All too often we see accountants advising investors to purchase negatively geared property. As we have noted, this can be a big mistake. Focusing purely on saving some tax is the opposite of setting up a self-sustaining positive cash flow property portfolio. So if your accountant is not on board with your long-term investment strategy, it might be time to look for a new one.

We are pleased to report, though, that nowhere near as many accountants push clients towards the negative gearing model these days compared to 10 years ago. We like using accountants who are also property investors because they understand the wealth-creation mindset, not just the tax-saving mindset.

Accountants charge an annual fee that depends on a few factors, such as how much the company charges, how many properties and loans you have, and whether they also manage your super. Their services can range between $300 and more than $5000. It really depends on the complexity of your personal and business finances.

Solicitor/conveyancer

Solicitors need to be quick-thinking, detail-oriented professionals who can add value to your due diligence process when transacting on a property. We like using solicitors who have been in the game for a while. The more experience they have, the better they can manoeuvre around problems that crop up during the purchase process.

Solicitors need to be tough, but not too tough. We have seen many solicitors representing either the buyer or the seller get too demanding. This can cause conflict and make the transaction more difficult. Remember, we are just trying to purchase a property. It's not a litigation process. Time and time again we have seen this happen, and it can actually hinder the negotiations if one side of the transaction starts to get frustrated or aggressive. When everyone works together amicably there is more flexibility for buyers.

For commercial purchases, we recommend that you use a qualified solicitor rather than just a conveyancer. This is because if you ever need to chase something up legally, you have an experienced solicitor ready to stand up for your rights.

Their costs will be anywhere from $1000 to $3500, and higher value commercial properties will attract higher fees. It's good practice to ask your solicitor for an estimate of the conveyancing transaction costs, so you know the total cost.

YOUR TAKEAWAYS

It's easier and wiser to outsource to people who know their stuff. But you should still do the legwork, so you understand fully what's happening within your portfolio.

Imagine managing tax time for 30-odd properties and even more tenancies! If you don't know everything that's going on, it's going to be hard to move forward, especially if things go pear-shaped.

Your best way forward is to be organised. Keep a file for each property and everything relating to it. And never throw documents out. We have found ourselves unable to claim things on properties through tax because we have mislaid or thrown out the supporting documentation.

If you're organised, have a long-term mindset and engage the right support team who are aligned with your goals, you are much more likely to achieve them.

STEP 3
ASSET SELECTION

Let's recap where we're at on your property journey. You have your deposit, and you have developed good money habits, including a buffer to cater for unanticipated costs that often crop up. You have sharpened your investment mindset and developed the right strategy and head space so you dedicate the time needed to wheel and deal in the commercial property market. You are now ready to take the next step—choosing the right property.

At this point, your priority is to understand the market, because as with any investment, success is all about buying the right type of asset at the right time and price. Luckily, you have a mountain of great resources at your disposal. Scan the newspapers for economic news, read investment magazines and the paper's property sections so you get to know what's happening in the market. If you're developing a passion for property, chances are you are already doing this, but we can't emphasise enough how important it is to do your research and get to know the market well before you do anything further.

Of course, this is easier said than done. The amount of information available can seem overwhelming. But you need to understand the whole picture so you can work out what drives the market.

It's worth noting that most of the properties advertised on the web won't stack up once you have carried out all your due diligence. It takes time, energy and dedication to pick out the good opportunities and the right commercial investments. For example, at Rethink Investing we review and reject about 30 properties for every single one we present to our clients.

To help you understand the market better, we recommend breaking down your research into smaller chunks.

Macroeconomics—the big picture

Macroeconomics is concerned with the broader aspects of national, regional or global markets and economic projections. When sourcing our properties, we first consider the big-picture stuff—including interest rates and government policies—because this gives broader context to our decisions. Then we drill down to developments at the micro level, such as infrastructure and local and state authorities' plans for the region. Your best sources of all this information are online global and economic data, daily newspapers and property publications. We also spend a fair bit of time researching the ASX these days to keep our finger on the pulse.

Here are a few of the larger macro-level forces that impact on the commercial property market:

- *Population.* For example, Australia's ageing baby boomer generation has increased demand for healthcare services such as aged-care facilities and medical centres, which will require increased federal government expenditure over the next few decades. It's worth considering how this may affect the market. Which suburbs will require more healthcare amenities and retail provisions? What are the main characteristics of the local population? Is it a relatively wealthy demographic with a high per-capita discretionary spend profile? Will strong population growth in areas undergoing gentrification require new services such as shopping centres, financial service companies and restaurants?

- *Infrastructure.* Are there government plans for new infrastructure? Infrastructure spending is an important growth driver. Big infrastructure projects can boost demand for commercial property. For instance, the development of the M7 in Sydney generated demand for warehouse properties in the surrounding precincts. We predict that over the next decade we will see the largest infrastructure boom we have ever seen. This will be one of the government's responses to stimulate growth in a post-COVID world.

- *Supply and demand.* You can look at the total number of building approvals nationwide as an early indicator of future supply. However, supply and demand is both a microeconomic and a macroeconomic driver of growth. For example, an increase in property within a specific suburb may create a threat, since the existing tenants may look to upgrade or expand. Which might cause you to lose your tenant and replace them at a lower rental rate. So, in general, you don't want a lot of new building in the precinct unless vacancy rates are very tight. Keeping on top of vacancy rates is one way to measure the health of the *supply and demand* ratio.

- *Interest rates* are one of the most important drivers for price valuations. When interest rates drop, investors are encouraged to take their money out of their bank accounts to seek higher returns elsewhere. By investing in commercial property, investor cash flow returns improve as the costs of lending drop. So what does this mean? Essentially, prices for commercial property increase because it's viable to pay more for the same rental return. This is called yield compression, which is how asset appreciation happens on a macro level.

To examine yield compression in a little more detail, let's look at the following example.

Let's say interest rates are 5 per cent and you purchase a $1.5 million property using a $1 million loan. That means an annual interest cost of $50 000 pa. If that $1 million loan is used to purchase a 7 per cent net yielding property, there will be a $55 000 net income after the cost of the debt has been accounted for (see table 13, overleaf).

Now let's look at the same situation if the interest rate dropped to 3 per cent. This would improve the net income on the commercial property from $55 000 to $75 000, which is a 36 per cent improvement in post-interest cash flow. Logically, therefore, investors would be encouraged to pay more for the property as the interest cost drops. This is called *yield compression.*

Table 13: yield compression

	Debt on property ($)	Cost of debt pa ($)	Net income for a $1.5 million asset ($)	Net income after debt repayments ($)	Cash flow improvement (%)
Interest rate 5%	1000000	50000	105000	55000	0
Interest rate 3%	1000000	30000	105000	75000	36

Vacancies

Understanding vacancy levels is very important, because it will help you secure a good deal on your commercial property. Your best preparation is to do your research. Consider how many vacant shops, offices, warehouses and factories there are in the precinct you are looking at. Also consider the exact length of the vacancies so you can work out how long it would take to relet your property. It's important to determine if they offer a true comparison to the property you're buying. For example, if you're looking to purchase a 500m² warehouse and there are seven other properties available to rent of over 2000m² each, this probably isn't an immediate threat to your property, because different tenants need different assets.

If there are many similar-sized, directly comparable vacancies, it could mean finding a new tenant will be difficult. If there are no vacancies, this is a good sign that the precinct is in high demand from businesses and that you are more likely to relet your property quickly. My advice is never to buy with vacant possession unless you are sure you can find a tenant quickly.

However, buying a property without a tenant may be viable if you can persuade the owner to guarantee at least 12 months' rent. This will give you time to find a tenant and might also allow you to buy at a lower price.

Where to invest

It may seem that we property investors have a knack for 'discovering' hidden gems that yield real estate gold. But the truth is, we have access to the same information you do; we're just across higher volumes of it. We know what to do with it too, and we have the contacts built up over years of experience to help us uncover the gold. It's also true that no one method delivers the best results; there are many. And it's worth knowing them all so you can use a good mix when you're ready to purchase.

It's also worth remembering that different types of commercial properties need different locations, so while there are opportunities all over Australia, I have always opted to invest in prime commercial locations. If you don't sacrifice on quality, you will always be able to attract the best tenants. This is because the best tenants always prefer the high-demand positions that attract the most foot traffic, access and prestige. For us, there is too much risk in heading to a sleepy little town just because the yield is good. As mentioned, however, large regional centres can be good investments as long as they are located near important infrastructure such as an airport, hospital or major highway, for example.

Location can make or break a business so, depending on your asset choice and your tenant type, you need to do a full market analysis on the viability of the tenant's business and the relettability of the property. When considering location, it's important to try to understand the growth drivers behind it. During an economic downturn, demand for certain types of commercial property generally falls due to sluggish economic growth and low business confidence. It's important to consider whether the investment may be susceptible to major economic downturns.

Let's drill down to understand more about the best reasons for choosing a property.

Visibility

In our eyes, highly visible equals highly attractive. And understanding the fundamentals of each asset class and their associated market is key.

So what constitutes good visibility across the various asset types in commercial property when it comes to choosing a location?

- *Office.* These spaces must be centrally situated and well serviced. It helps to have offices near retail amenities and transport networks, and to have adequate onsite car parking. Natural lighting and functional floor plates/tenancy areas are also important considerations; offices with only artificial light may be cheaper. Another value-add could be an aesthetically pleasing setting. For example, any Sydney office space with views of the harbour will demand a premium rent. Office investments can become riskier as they become dated, so make sure the aesthetic appeal is great enough to attract your tenant.

- *Industrial.* For these properties it's all about location and great access. The ability to transport materials and goods in and out of a site saves significant extra logistical costs. So industrial sites close to major arterial roads and rail access are highly attractive. Proximity to an airport or seaport will also increase a property's attractiveness to prospective tenants.

- *Retail.* The most important factor to consider when investing in the retail market is foot traffic. Look for places where people regularly congregate in high volumes, because more people means more opportunities for business and generating sales. You also need to consider the tenant mix of the area. For example, you wouldn't want too many Thai restaurants close to one another. Also, look for exposure to passing traffic, anchor tenants such as supermarkets and a good customer car parking ratio.

Parking

Adequate parking is important for both customers and staff, especially when you are buying in built-out urban areas where space is scarce. For example, if you buy an office space a high ratio of parking spaces to total square metres will add significantly to the property's value. This is because it makes the property more attractive to tenants and you'll be able to fill the property faster while also chasing a premium rent. Car parking is particularly important in the retail sector where customers need to carry purchases to their cars. Retail businesses or those with a retail component also need exposure, so main-road frontage within an established commercial precinct can be critical to the success of a business—and to your chances of securing a tenant. You can also rent car parks out separately for a secondary revenue source.

The building/layout

Consider the structure or 'bones' of the property and whether the layout can be easily changed to suit different types of tenants. It's important to consider properties that can be configured differently, because a multi-purpose space can help you attract a wider pool of potential tenants by marketing the property to many types of tenants. And you won't be left with an inefficient floor layout if you sublease the space.

Industrial sites require great onsite access, plenty of space in which large vehicles can manoeuvre, good clearance height into the warehouse/factory and the right office-to-warehouse ratio. A good tip is to find an industrial site where the proportion of office space can easily be changed.

Check the build costs per square metre in the area and compare it to your building. Look for areas where you can buy a building below its replacement cost, as this means there will be less future competition for you from developers—until prices rise, that is!

Keep in mind that larger commercial properties may be more difficult to lease than smaller properties and will typically be more expensive to hold.

Get personal

If you can, walk around the area and call the commercial property agents who work in the area to check on rents. Meet up with them and ask them about their property listings. Read the newspaper property sections, search the web and subscribe to local agents' mailing lists. And investigate the health of the business sector you expect your tenant to come from.

Get familiar with this asset class. Expand your knowledge by talking to experts in the field. Ask them about the deals they've done in the past, and the type of properties they've bought. The agents in the areas are a fantastic source of information, and they are usually passionate about property. Ask them about recent sales and the listings they have coming up. It's also helpful to speak to other investors to help build your knowledge about the good and bad side of investing. Ultimately, this will give you the confidence to choose the right property.

If you don't have the time or ability to carry out this local research, this is where a buyer's agent can help fast-track your results.

The tenant

Finding the right tenant is an important part of the property deal. We only purchase and recommend leased investments, meaning the property is sold with the tenant already in place. In simple terms, having a tenant in place mitigates your risks and improves your chance of a good return as you can complete your due diligence on the tenant. This creates a lot more certainty when buying. And it makes financing easier.

We advise you to look for a strong corporate or blue-chip tenant, or any tenant with a long successful trading history, that has the financial resources to meet the rental payments and is unlikely to default on the rent, particularly when it is already in the location you are purchasing. Review the tenant's business model, brand assets, annual statements, resources and even industry trends to better assess their viability as a long-term tenant.

Other factors you should consider in relation to tenants include:

- *Who are they?* How long have they occupied the premises and is their rent up to date? We like to ask for bank statements that have the tenant's payment history clearly displayed, so we can see whether they have paid their rent on time each month. It's important to note when the lease expires. For example, some multiple-tenant assets may have all their leases expire in the same year. Although not a deal breaker, it adds to the risk.

- *Best tenants.* They have a good track record in business or are the type of business that has good growth potential. For example, solicitors and accountants have shown substantial durability over the years and have a public image of reliability and responsibility.

Check out Property Play 3 for more details on the types of tenants we recommend.

- *Lease length.* Leases are typically for three to five years, with tenants paying all the outgoings, often including the managing agent's fees. Sometimes you can buy shorter leases to secure the property for a lower price (due to the extra risk). Once you increase the lease, you can then create value on the asset you purchase—extra risk plus extra upside.

- *Rent price.* Make sure the tenant is paying a fair market rent. This is extremely important as the commercial property can be valued from its rental income. If the rent is inflated, then you might be offering too much, and you will have little upside potential for rent reviews and therefore increased capital values.

- *Below-market rent.* Finding below-market rent is also a way of identifying future value-add properties, because you can potentially raise the rent at the next rent review to match it to market level. When done correctly, this will increase your equity.

- *Lease structure.* This includes the length of the lease, the frequency and methods of rent review, and who pays the operating costs. Of course, it's preferable to have a long lease with regular rent reviews to market with a minimum of CPI increase and a tenant who pays all the outgoings.

- *Relettability.* Many investors forget the importance of the property's relettability. No matter how good or secure your tenant looks, it's prudent to consider how you would go about finding a new tenant, because you never know what the future will bring.

Where are they?

Finding a suitable new tenant can be a challenging. And just as with valuing a property, working out a vacancy period is vital. But we've been doing it for years, and over time we've developed some great tactics, including:

- *CoreLogic.* Find the leasing history of similar properties in the area by searching the extensive CoreLogic property website. For example, if you are looking at a 300m² warehouse, research vacant units sized between 200m² and 400m², and see how long it took to fill them. If in most cases the vacancy was between two and three months, we would allow for a three-month vacancy when looking for a tenant.

- *Local rental managers.* If you don't know the area well, speak with local rental managers to confirm your findings. A local leasing specialist who is active in the area and experienced in your particular type of asset not only knows what tenants are new to the area and actively looking, but knows the tenants who are already operating, when their lease expires and their requirements. So if their current premises no longer meets their demands, they may be able to move them across to something bigger, smaller or more suitable—such as *your* property.

YOUR TAKEAWAYS

It's hard to know where to start when searching for the right property. There's such a lot of information out there! We have invested tens of thousands of hours in studying the art of real estate in order to learn what works and what doesn't.

In the search for the best commercial properties, nothing beats knowledge combined with experience. Whether it's reading printed and online resources, or carrying out on-the-ground research, your best strategy is to research and understand the key drivers and influences on the market and the broader economy, and the way they impact specific properties and tenancies.

METHOD OF SALE

Lining up your finance and completing your due diligence are huge steps towards securing your commercial property, but you also need to know how the property will be brought to the market. There are different ways to buy a property, depending on how it's marketed, and you need to know what boxes to tick when it comes to your due diligence.

Your first step is to learn the different methods of sale of commercial property. As touched on earlier, most of us are familiar with the different ways to buy a residential property. It's not too different for commercial property, but there are more variations in sales methods. Generally, these assets are sold through expression of interest campaigns, auctions and (increasingly) off-market sales. Your competition may include individuals, trusts, companies or even syndicates.

In the commercial market, the range of methods of sale are:

1. auctions
2. EOI (expressions of interest)
3. fixed-price listings
4. off-market sales.

Let's break these down.

1. Auctions

As in the residential sector, auctions are usually preferred for properties that are likely to be in high demand, especially in the capital cities. That's why you'll find that auctions are typical for any commercial building in Melbourne's or Sydney's CBD, because the agent knows that demand will be high and active bidding will push the price up for the seller.

In an auction, the seller may allow for some flexibility in the bidding and purchasing terms, which the auctioneer will announce prior to the auction. Keep in mind that purchasing terms at an auction are usually dictated by the seller rather than the buyer in a hot market. All of this reduces your control when buying and is more likely to lead you to overpay or lead to a costly oversight.

This is why we advise you to avoid this type of auction scenario. In our general business, we prefer to stick to other methods of sale where you're more likely to get value for money and the sort of profit that will be harder to achieve for highly attractive and highly competitive properties.

In Australia, auctions for commercial properties typically account for about 20 per cent of sales. We dislike them when representing clients mainly because we can't negotiate favourable due diligence or finance terms. Most auctions also demand an unconditional contract, which can be risky. But there is a bit of a silver lining: if you rock up to an auction where there is little interest, it will really show you where the market stands. You might then try to purchase the property after the auction with all your due diligence and finance conditions covered.

Our auction top tips

Make sure you do your homework if you're going down this path, because in the heat of an auction you need to know exactly what you're doing. We've bought commercial properties at many auctions and have learned to keep a cool head. This will probably be nothing you haven't heard before, but what's critical is that you have all your ducks lined up properly. This means having your finances in tiptop order, because when you buy a commercial property at auction, you'll need to organise your bank's unconditional approval beforehand. This can take a few weeks to arrange and cost several thousand dollars, so if you don't win at the auction it's a bitter pill to swallow—and potentially a big waste of money.

You'll have to have your 10 per cent deposit ready to go if you win it. If you don't have it, you might be able to negotiate a lower deposit with the seller's solicitor even before the auction. Be aware that if you have to use other properties as security, you may be stung with higher interest rates for those borrowings until the finance is settled.

Once the hammer comes down and you've still got your hand stuck in the air, the property's yours. And that means making sure you've done all your due diligence before the day of the auction.

2. Expressions of interest (EOIs)

An expression of interest is generally far less of a pressure cooker situation for many than an auction, mainly because you don't have to look your competition in the eye and there is more time to work with. With an EOI, you simply submit your offer, which isn't binding. EOIs allow buyers to specify their preferred purchasing terms, then it's up to the seller to decide if they are acceptable or if they want to negotiate further. Note that an EOI is still bound by its own rules—notably, that you'll have to enter a bid by a certain due date and you'll need to abide by the closing date. So in a way you're just putting off the inevitable price war, only it's invisible because you won't know who you're up against.

If you're headed down this path, you'll be asked to fill out a standard EOI form. It's only one or two pages and is pretty similar across the various commercial property agencies. The most important point made in the form is that you don't need to do all of your due diligence straightaway, as you have to in the auction process. You are required only to indicate how much time you'll need to get this done, because at this stage you're simply registering your interest in the property.

Once the closing date arrives, which could be up to six weeks down the track, the agent will call you to chat about the next step—the wheeling and dealing.

Our EOI top tips

At this point, the vendor's agent hasn't yet had to work for their money. They've let the expressions of interest roll in, and they've had time to sort out the wheat from the chaff. You'll most likely hear one or more of the following lines, which they love to trot out to up the ante and drum up excitement:

- 'You've made a solid start, but you'll need to come up a little to be in line with the vendor's expectations.'

- 'Another, similar offer has come in. I recommend you put your best foot forward on price.'

- 'The owner is still considering the offers. All I can say is you will need to be over the XX price.'

- 'The vendor will be making a decision over the weekend. I recommend putting in your best price before 5 pm Friday.'

One great thing about EOIs is that you can negotiate on things other than price. You might be able to offer a better deal on the settlement conditions, so it's worth making sure you have some wiggle room in your first offer so you have some bargaining power during the negotiations. Our offers will vary depending on the type of property. Some vendors will be won over on price, some on settlement conditions, some on both. Here are a few examples of these conditions:

- Most commercial offers are made with a 21-day due diligence or finance condition. If you are prepared to shorten this, it will give you more leverage on the offer.

- Most commercial contracts are for 42–60 days. Again, if you can go shorter, this will give you more leverage.

- Larger deposits help. If you are feeling super-confident in the property, you might even offer a non-refundable amount (but this is not something we often do).

- Find out if the vendor has any other preferences you can work into your offer. (In some cases they may even want a longer settlement.)

3. Fixed-price listings

In this method, what you see is what you get. Pure and simple. The owner knows what price they want, the agent lists it, and it's there in black and white for the market to buy or pass on. The process is open and transparent too. To get to this point, there's been a significant amount of research into the listing price, and for many investors buying this way saves a lot of time and energy stuffing around with banks and other institutions.

Think of it as a bit like the opposite of an auction. Properties that are sold under this method are usually listed because the demand isn't high. They may have been passed in at auction or listed with another agent. Developers often use fixed prices to lock in a certain amount of profit margin, otherwise it's not worth selling. Do your due diligence to find out if there's any existing selling history so you don't pay more than you should.

It's also worth remembering that when an agent lists a fixed price, the owner has not had to outlay much on a marketing campaign. Reading between the lines, this is usually because they don't expect interest to be that high. For an informed investor—which you will be—there's gold to be found in these listings, so don't dismiss them!

Fixed-price top tips

The key is to make sure you still complete your due diligence on the price. Look for comparable sales and back yourself in valuing the property without being influenced by the listing price. If the deal stacks up at their asking price, then great. If not, on you go to the next deal.

Before you move on, though, it's always worth trying to offer a lower price where you see value. Try to find out as much as you can about the property, so you have some bargaining power. Again, offer a quicker settlement if it's possible and see if you can find out if the vendor has other motivations for selling.

In fixed-price sales, don't wait too long if you are hoping the owner will hold out for you.

4. Off-market sales

This one's our favourite. The longer you're in this game, the more likely you'll be the person agents call when they have a property that isn't going to be listed on the market. And you can catch a great deal this way! Because they know you, trust you and appreciate that you're a professional, you're more likely to get a deal when something good comes along.

With an off-market sale, the owner doesn't list or advertise the property and may be in a hurry to sell. The agent will use their networks to see who might be interested to buy and will go about marketing it privately between prospective buyers.

There are a few reasons why a seller chooses to sell off-market:

- *Privacy.* They might not wish anyone to know they are selling.

- *Protect tenants.* Fewer inspections and questions can help keep their tenants happy.

- *Cheaper.* Discreet advertising campaigns are the cheapest (no professional photos, costly auctions and so on).

- *Speed.* Sometimes an agent needs to approach only one buyer to make the sale. This can mean much faster results compared to a drawn-out marketing campaign.

How do you access off-market properties?

For the investor, it's all about building your networks. It can take many years to reach a point where you are regularly alerted to high-quality off-market opportunities. We completed literally thousands commercial purchases for ourselves and our clients, which results in reaching out to countless numbers of agents and regularly improving our relationships with them. The consequence of this is getting to know the main players in the game, to understand who's who in the zoo, and that means knowing who has access to the best off-market stock. One of the most valuable assets a professional investor can have is their network.

Our off-market sales top tips

This process follows much the same path as we've covered, but this time you'll likely be under time pressure to buy the property before it is presented to another buyer or listed online. As with any sale, the vendor's agent will try to negotiate the best deal for their client. They may point out how very lucky and privileged you are to have been given this opportunity, which may sometimes be true, but in other cases, where the quality is poor, be ready to walk away if it doesn't meet your standards. Remember, being an off-line deal doesn't necessarily mean it's going to be a good one. So, as always, do the numbers and calculate what you need to secure a good deal.

Over the years, about 60 per cent of the properties we have bought have been off-market deals. This is one of the key ways we position ourselves as experts. We have access to properties before they hit the market, giving us first dibs on the best ones. You need to act with confidence on price and be ready to justify your offer by understanding the market, the property, the rent and the rate of return.

Your access to off-market properties will increase if you complete sales regularly. Unfortunately, this is a privilege reserved mainly for buyer's agents who purchase frequently on behalf of their clients. If you purchase many properties from the same agents, you become their 'go to' buyer for quick sales. This is something we have perfected over the years in our business.

If operating only on your own behalf, you need to give the agent confidence you are a legit buyer, someone who can navigate the transaction smoothly and easily. If you sell yourself as a buyer in the right way, the agent will keep you in the loop with other off-market deals. If this is something you would like to shortcut, then engaging a buyer's agent with good contacts will allow you to leverage off their networks without having to build your own from scratch.

YOUR TAKEAWAYS

There are several ways to buy property, but if we were to leave you with just one tip, it would be to try to take back control from the selling agent. It's in the agent's best interests to control as much of the process as they can, so the more you can see what is happening during the sales process, the more likely you are to walk away with a good deal. Being educated about the market and the property itself is the best way to gain confidence and hence control over the negotiations.

Of course, you might not always like the selling method, but as long as the numbers stack up, and you are happy to proceed within the agreed parameters, then go for it!

Build good relationships with commercial real estate agents and you'll be in their thoughts when the best properties hit the market. Ultimately, this is what you want to aim for. Get the deals before they reach the online listings and you'll know you're onto a good thing!

FINANCE

Property investing is often described as a game of finance. When financing property deals we believe investors should always use loans, even if they have the cash to buy the property outright. Why? A simple reason: you can maximise your returns better by using bank finance. It's called *leveraging*.

Leveraging has the additional advantage of allowing you to front up with less cash when buying a property. This puts you in a great position to buy multiple properties, which translates into more income sources and more diversity as you grow your portfolio. We wouldn't be in the position we're in without using loans!

Let's look at how your returns can be increased by using the bank's money rather than buying a property outright.

CASE STUDY
Cash versus bank loan

A client of ours, James, came to us with approximately $500 000 in cash savings. He was set against taking out a bank loan as he viewed lending as riskier than using cash, and he believed he had enough to purchase a small commercial property outright. We compared the numbers for buying a property outright versus splitting his $500 000 between three commercial properties, using 70 per cent bank loans.

Let's see how it pans out.

Scenario 1: James purchases a $450 000 property outright.
- $30 000 covers purchasing costs (stamp duty, legals and so on)
- $20 000 is kept as a buffer for the property against unanticipated expenses.

Potential result when purchasing an asset with a 7 per cent net return:
- $31500 pa rent (tenant pays 100 per cent of the property's outgoings)

- Bank loan = $0

- **Total return = $31500 per annum + capital growth.**

Scenario 2: James purchases three properties for $400000 each using a 70 per cent loan.
- $120000 for each 30 per cent deposit on a $400000 property

- $25000 to cover purchasing costs for each property (total: $75000)

- $65000 as a buffer for the properties.

Potential result when purchasing an asset with a 7 per cent net return:
- The three properties rent for a combined amount of $84000 rent (tenant pays 100 per cent of the property's outgoings)

- Bank loan = $840000

- Interest rate = 3.5 per cent interest only

- **Total return = $54600 per annum + capital growth.**

As you can see, leveraging your money will increase your cash flow returns much more for commercial property. It's also important to note that owning $1200000 in real estate (James's three properties) will increase your chances of accumulating better capital growth over a long period than owning only $450000.

For example, if your $450000 property grows 5 per cent per annum for 10 years, its value will increase by $248097.70. But taking that same growth rate, your $1200000 portfolio will grow by $661593.86 — a whopping $413496.16 difference. And that's simply because you took out a bank loan 10 years earlier.

Table 14 compares the growth (assumed at 5 per cent per annum) over 10 years for the two scenarios.

Table 14: growth comparison over 10 years of two investment scenarios

Assumption of 5% pa growth	$450 000 property	3 x $400 000 properties
Value Year 1	$450 000.00	$1 200 000.00
Value Year 2	$472 500.00	$1 260 000.00
Value Year 3	$496 125.00	$1 323 000.00
Value Year 4	$520 931.25	$1 389 150.00
Value Year 5	$546 977.81	$1 458 607.50
Value Year 6	$574 326.70	$1 531 537.88
Value Year 7	$603 043.04	$1 608 114.77
Value Year 8	$633 195.19	$1 688 520.51
Value Year 9	$664 854.95	$1 772 946.53
Value Year 10	$698 097.70	$1 861 593.86
Total growth	**$248 097.70**	**$661 593.86**
	Difference	$413 496.16

There are other benefits to leveraging. In this case, James will have three assets with three different tenants in three different suburbs/areas. This diversity reduces his vacancy risk, because the chance that all three tenancies would be vacant at once is probably slim.

Also, the flexibility in scenario 2 means James can sell one of the assets if he needs to while still receiving an income, and he can cash out for whatever reason. If, however, he owned only one commercial property and had to sell, he would lose all his income there and then. This case study illustrates how important it is to get the finance right from the start, and how the game is to get the best result possible for your personal situation.

Starting out

Of course, as a skilled investor, you must consider many other factors when borrowing. There are a bunch of rules that you need to be across too. Understanding them, and knowing where and when you can take shortcuts or give yourself a better chance, will allow you to get ahead of the game, legally and credibly. Without this knowledge, it will be harder to build a large, self-sustaining property portfolio.

One of the reasons we've been able to generate such a large portfolio is that right from the start we were very good at maximising our lending capacity.

But first, to get you on your way, here's what you need to do.

Save a deposit

We covered this in Step 1, so we won't spend too long on it here. Suffice to say that every property deal, whether residential or commercial, starts with a deposit. In Part I we talked you through recommended deposit amounts if you're buying commercial property; if you're in this boat, we suggest you aim to save a ballpark $100000. Of course, if you're pulling equity from other properties you won't need to save as much, but you will need cash, so you should still aim for this amount.

If you came into this thinking that you're nowhere near the ballpark figure, don't worry. Our best advice is simply to turn around, focus on saving and bringing that figure a little closer. If you don't, you'll simply waste your time at the bank trying to justify finance, and they'll tell you exactly the same thing.

Alternatively, if you've done the hard yards and got your savings in order, then read on. Saving up for a deposit is usually the hardest and most time-consuming part of the game. Once you're there you're ready to start shopping.

Table 15 illustrates the deposit you should aim for commensurate with the property price.

Table 15: deposit needed per property value

Property value	30% deposit + 5% costs*
$300 000	$105 000
$500 000	$175 000
$700 000	$245 000
$900 000	$315 000
$1 100 000	$385 000
$1 300 000	$455 000
$1 500 000	$525 000
$1 700 000	$595 000
$1 900 000	$665 000
$2 100 000	$735 000
$2 300 000	$805 000
$2 500 000	$875 000

* A 5 per cent allowance for purchasing costs will cover stamp duty, solicitor fees, building/pest report and so on.

Give yourself a buffer

There's nothing worse than feeling pleased that you've saved your deposit only to be slugged by unanticipated extra costs. That's why we recommend giving yourself a buffer, so when those extra costs pop up—and they will—you can cover them from your reserve.

Here are a few examples of extra fees and charges to keep an eye out for:

- *Bank costs.* Banks may charge fees you aren't expecting. They might even ask for a larger deposit at the last minute before settlement, in some unlucky cases.

- *An early, unexpected vacancy.* For example, when COVID-19 hit, gyms were forced to close, which meant tenants couldn't pay the rent in full, leaving owners with a short-term cash flow problem.

- *Valuation shortfall.* If the bank valuation comes back lower than the purchase price, you will have to pay the difference. For example, if you have a valuation returned at $50 000 below the purchase price, you can either challenge the valuation, pay the difference or try to renegotiate the price with the vendor.

- *Maintenance.* Although in most cases the tenants are required to pay for the maintenance of the property, it's still good practice to have a buffer in place.

Remember, your best defence is to plan for the worst. Get that buffer up and you'll be more likely to breeze through these little interruptions. We recommend adding a cushion of 10 per cent. Don't even think of it as a buffer; imagine it's just part of your deposit and you won't even notice the little extra you need to save. Trust us, it's much better to factor this in than to stress about having to scrounge around for money you don't necessarily have, especially when on a deadline.

Loan structure and application process

The loan structure for a commercial property is different from that for a residential property. Given that you probably won't be buying your commercial property outright, understanding this is important. But how do you know what to look out for? If you're just getting started in commercial property investment, it might look daunting.

In essence, the banks will be looking at a few key criteria, including:

- your ability to repay the loan. They'll consider all your income, which will include what you're expecting to receive from the commercial property.

- how much deposit you have, and if you have any equity to use from another property.

- what type of commercial property you wish to buy, its location and the valuer's report.

- the commercial property lease and its conditions.

If you have all the above in order, you're ready to hit the banks. But how do you choose between them? What do you look for? Here are our tips on getting to grips with the application process and loan structure.

Big banks versus specialised lenders

Things can be easier if you engage a mortgage broker with commercial lending experience, rather than securing the loan yourself from one of the big four banks. That's because a broker will have access to a wider range of lending options, including non-bank lenders. Often these lenders are more competitive than the big banks, which means you'll find a better deal.

Shorter loan terms

Residential loans are typically for 25 to 30 years. Commercial loans can range from short-term loans of a year to 10 years all the way up to 30 years. It's important to note that the shorter the term the faster the loan must be paid back. As a consequence, you'll need to be able to convince the lender that you can service the loan, because the repayments will be higher.

A rule of thumb is the longer the loan terms, the better the serviceability. This is because the buffering test of repayments will be stretched out over a longer time period. So if you can get longer term loans, this will be a better result for your serviceability.

Lender's policy

The rate, terms and structure are very similar across all lenders. Where they differ is in their policies and varying tools, and the way you can make them work in a deal. Let's go through a few of them, because understanding these can mean the difference between securing a great deal or missing out.

Here are some examples to look out for:

- Some banks can do standalone deals, which can help with serviceability.
- Rental shading. Some banks only consider 70 per cent of the income instead of 100 per cent. In some cases it can be even less,

such as 65 per cent or 50 per cent. The stronger the rental shading the harder it is to get a loan, because the figures show you have less income to support your loan.

- Lenders that allow interest addbacks for servicing, net profit addbacks.

- Postcode restrictions, which can result in the loan being denied.

- First-time use. This is a new one I've just started to see pop up. Basically, the banks offer different loan terms for new properties than for older ones.

- Retail/office/industrial. These types of commercial properties can have different LVRs, reflecting their differing risk levels.

- Loan size limits. As you borrow more you will encounter different policies for different levels of debt. This is one reason why many larger investors spread their loans across multiple banks.

The property

The property itself can be a factor when it comes to commercial finance. Its location, security, tenant and lease terms are major determinants of the maximum LVR (loan-to-value ratio) and in some cases the actual rate for the borrower. It's worth keeping this in mind when you're searching for your property, because it can make the difference between good finance and great finance. Given that the LVR is generally lower for commercial properties (70 per cent, compared to 80–90 per cent for residential property), you'll also need a bigger deposit or more equity.

Strategic lease terms

You might be in a better position to secure your loan by playing around with the lease terms. This is something we often do for Rethink Investing clients when we put offers on properties. We make them subject to a lease negotiation. Commercial leases offer much more flexibility than residential leases, which means there's plenty of room for negotiation. For example, a typical residential lease is six to 12 months. A commercial lease, on the other hand, is usually longer. This might include an ongoing 3+3 years or 5+5 years with options to extend for another three to five years. Tenants usually pay their own outgoings. Basically, all these items are negotiable, but the better the negotiation goes for you, the more favourably the lease is for the lender. If the lease is strong enough you might be able to get a *lease doc loan*—that is, a loan on the property purely from the income on the lease without taking into account your personal income. This is a good type of loan for those who have reached their serviceability limits.

Property valuation

You'll need to pay for a lender's valuation on your commercial property. If you've bought residential property, this cost is usually covered by the lender, but in commercial loan applications, it's up to you to foot the bill.

To give you an idea of the cost, anything under $1 million will cost around $800 to $1500. If the property is valued at over $1 million, the cost will be higher. There may also be an additional GST cost.

The good news is these detailed valuations are an important part of your due diligence. Although they are often based on the most conservative of views, they can still give you great market insights to boost your confidence in your commercial purchase decision.

Principal and interest (P&I) or interest only loans

You will need to work out whether P&I or interest only is better suited to your circumstances. Personally, we choose P&I on our home loan but interest only on our investment loans. It's worth remembering that investment loans are tax deductible, but your home loan isn't. So it's better from a tax point of view to maximise your investment loans and reduce your home loan.

Let's look at an example. If you choose P&I, you'll be able to secure higher lending because the stress testing of repayments is based on the remaining loan term. So if you have a 20-year commercial loan with five years interest only, the remaining P&I term will be 15 years. The lender will then say that the balance is to be repaid over 15 years on the stress-tested rate. This commonly kills a lot of deals. However, if you opt for P&I, it's 20 years stress test on the balance instead of 15 years.

One positive advance in recent times is that banks are offering much longer loan terms for commercial loans. Most of our clients secure 25- to 30-year commercial loans these days. This helps their serviceability, so they can keep buying!

Other options

There are a few reasons why things don't work out when financing. If all the above fails, you can look at a lease doc or a standalone approach.

For a lease doc loan, the lender only looks at the commercial property you are purchasing for servicing and ignores all your other financials.

For a standalone loan, the lender only looks at the financials of the entity you are purchasing. For example, if it's a family trust entity, only the financials of the family trust will be considered; if it's a company, then the financials of the company will be the lender's only concern.

YOUR TAKEAWAYS

In commercial property, the interest rate is only one consideration. Borrowers have a bunch of other factors at their disposal to help them grow a larger commercial property portfolio.

Sometimes it's worth paying that higher rate to secure the investment. Sure, it might cost a little more (which is tax deductible), but in the longer term the investment will pay dividends and provide growth that will quickly outstrip that small cost.

The best advice we can offer here is that you make sure you have an expert commercial broker on your team. Once you do, you can basically automate all the advice/information reviewed in this chapter.

THE NEGOTIATIONS

If you've got this far, well done! You've done the searching and due diligence, and you've sorted out your finances. All that's left to do is to seal the deal. You are now ready to start the negotiations to secure your commercial property.

In residential property, this is relatively straightforward. Head to the auction, stick up your hand and the property's yours. Or negotiate a private sale. One title, one sale. In commercial property, things can be trickier. What if the property sits on several titles? There may be multiple leases too, with various tenants on different terms and agreements, plus potential vacancies to deal with.

It can sometimes take weeks or even months before agreement is reached and the contract of sale is signed. This is because from your first, non-binding expression of interest, you will need to negotiate the terms of the deal and be confident enough to deliver your best offer.

There's a great saying in real estate investing: 'You make your money when you buy, not when you sell.' Your purchase price is the main determinant of your ultimate profit. So how do you secure the right purchase price? Three important factors: understanding how the sales process works, understanding the current market conditions and understanding your real estate agent. Get these factors right and you'll be signing on the dotted line in no time.

Negotiating a good deal

Being a good negotiator is key to getting the best results. How do you negotiate the best deal? After personally negotiating over $1 billion in completed sales, and losing many more, here are our best tips when going into any negotiation.

Do your homework

You need to make sure you know the market, the value and the vendor's expectations before putting down an offer. Don't throw in a ridiculously lowball offer, as the only thing this will achieve is make you look uneducated on the market. Commercial sellers don't respond well to crazy lowball offers either, so it might hurt your chances of being taken seriously in the negotiations. When you know the real value of the property, you'll be able to bid with confidence and respond to the seller with authority. This will fast-track the negotiations in your favour.

A quick starting point on how to value a property is knowing the market rent value. If you're negotiating with the selling agent yourself, here are a few questions to ask about the current rent that will help you value the property:

- What is the current rent for the property?
- What is the rent for comparable properties nearby?
- What is the median market rent in the area as a whole?

By now you'll be very aware of the value we place on *doing your homework*. Maybe not in school, but definitely in real estate! To set the baseline of any negotiations, we want to know as much as we can about the property, who's selling it and their motivation for selling it. The best way to do this is to draw on your experience of that market, or if you are new to the area, to quickly fill in any knowledge gaps you may have. If you can manage it, a site visit can prove very useful.

If it's a retail property, this is even easier, because you can walk into the shop and have a chat with whoever is behind the register. If it's a building with several tenants, you can pop in and have a chat with the people who work there. Whether it's the owner or an employee, try to find out as much as you can. The question you really want answered is why are they selling? They may be reluctant to answer directly, but you'll get better at this with practice. If, for example, you learn that the owner is relocating overseas, this will open up your negotiating options, because they'll probably be under pressure to sell before they leave.

Here are a few other questions you might ask:

- How long have you been running your business here?
- When are your busiest times?
- What maintenance has been done to the property over the tenancy?
- What is the area like?
- What other businesses are operating in your building/area?
- Are there any vacancies nearby?
- Do you think you will be here for a while? (That one can be a little direct so make sure the conversation is going well before asking it.)

Have a look around the area too. Check out any other shops or businesses nearby. What sort of condition is the building in? Every scrap of information is useful and adds to your negotiating power, so dig around.

Take emotion out of the equation

We talked about this earlier in the book, but it's worth reiterating. Far too often we see people fall in love with a property and pay too much. Or worse, we see people get frustrated on a personal level with an agent, vendor or prospective buyer, and want to walk away on 'principle'. (I confess this is also one of my personal weaknesses, which I have had to learn to control! — Scott.) Emotions are not helpful to your efforts and have no place in negotiating a good deal.

This is where a buyer's agent can be invaluable because they have no emotional connection to the property or the principals. This means the negotiations will come down to the last $5000 or $10000, and an expert negotiator will hold out and not pay the difference.

Become a good listener

Being a good listener has served us well over our 1800-plus successful property negotiations. This means listening closely to what the vendor says. Sometimes a faster settlement may be needed, and we can work with that. Sometimes the vendor needs help understanding the true market value, and we can also help with that by showing them comparable sales. Sometimes the vendor needs more time to consider the offer as they are not yet ready to accept a lower amount—yep, that too. Always listen to what they have to say, because your next move may well depend on it. Good communications may also help you in the future with the same vendor, especially if they remember you were great to work with.

Remember to always keep your cool. When it looks as though the deal is done, but not in your favour, don't lose your temper. Settle down and think about a solution that might benefit everyone. The great thing about commercial deals is that you can negotiate on a range of factors. Consider, for example, the interior of the premises, the number and location of car parking spaces, whether the lease could include extra spaces on the premises for the tenant's use, the number of years on the lease and how many extra years you could add on at renewal. But more on that later.

Don't give anything away without getting something in return

Whenever we give something away, we expect to see some sort of compromise from the vendor. Think of it as the give and take of business dealing. If you give something away without any matching flexibility by the vendor, there's the risk that they will feel entitled to your concession and will not be satisfied until you have given further ground. On the other hand, if they've had to work a little bit to earn their return, it'll give them a greater sense of pride and satisfaction than if they had earned it without having to do anything.

Negotiate in good faith

This is a big one for us. We like investing with the goal of creating a win/win solution. After all, a deal will never be made if both parties don't agree on a final position. This is why we like to make sensible offers that work for us, and then make sure we understand what the sellers need for the deal to work for them. With no emotional distraction, no-one is offended or frustrated with the process. If you can work like this, more deals will go in your favour. Someone who wants to 'crush' the sellers into submission with a very lowball offer is a poor negotiator. Trying to defeat the other party is not the attitude you should go in with. Negotiations are not wars; they are pathways to a mutual agreement. Work with the sellers and they will work with you. This is how we have negotiated all our best deals.

The deal structure

During negotiations there are many angles you can play. Think carefully about how the components of any deal will affect your longer term outcomes, then come up with a solution that's a win/win for everyone.

Think, for example, of a sale negotiation and leaseback scenario (which can occur when the tenant and the owner are the same person). Should you reduce the rent to help lower the asking price? On the face of it, it might seem as though dropping the rent would be a good option, because you're not losing any money from your own pocket if you are getting it back in the sale price. But the lower rent may also lower your valuation for years to come.

With this in mind, here is a list of the most common aspects of a deal that can be negotiated:

- rental income (for leasebacks)
- rental guarantees
- shorter or longer settlements
- maintenance and repairs allowances
- a discount on sale price
- works undertaken (for example, if you attach a physical mezzanine level to the building).

These are all items we regularly seek to bring into a negotiation where applicable.

CASE STUDY
Client purchase in 2020

This investment, which settled for one of our clients in mid-2020, is an example of how many layers there are in some negotiations.

We were presented with this property off-market in February. The vendor sought offers over $1 300 000. Although this was a pretty decent deal, we knew we wanted it for around $1 250 000.

We offered $1 200 000, which was a pretty big lowball offer by our standards. It wasn't received too well, and the negotiations stalled there. The owners really wanted $1 350 000. Weeks later the property was online, then COVID-19 hit Australia. Most of us in the industry took a back seat in March to wait to see what would happen. By mid April the signs were looking better than expected and most states saw buyer demand increase sharply. We were back, and still interested in this property.

Now there was more economic uncertainty, though, and we wanted more out of the deal. So we offered the same money ($1 200 000) with a 12-month rental guarantee on top of the lease. Again this was rejected, but interestingly the vendor's expectations had softened. Now they were at $1275000 with a six-month rental guarantee.

Another few weeks passed and after a lot of back and forth we finally agreed on terms:

- Purchase price: $1250000
- Terms: 21 days for due diligence and 21 days for finance approval
- Settlement: 35 days
- Extra: 12-month rental guarantee.

So after a long couple of months we were under contract with a property we saw a lot of value in, especially as a 5+5-year lease with a 12-month rental guarantee was included, which meant double-backed rent.

But the deal was not yet done. The next part was to complete a building and pest inspection, and we discovered that the build had issues. There was a leak in the roof, which was a body corporate issue. So we asked the vendor to fix the problem. They said they had fixed it. Then it rained, and we reinspected it. And guess what? It was still leaking.

We asked again, and this time it was harder to get proof that the leak had been fixed, as it would need to rain hard again to confirm it. So, rather than leave it to Lady Luck, we asked for a 12-month maintenance guarantee on the roof leak. The vendors graciously agreed, and the solicitors drew up the legal paperwork. The property settled a month later.

As you can see there are many things you can negotiate, but you can also take advantage of the market conditions at the same time. It was all about getting the best result for the buyer, but the vendor was also happy with the result.

YOUR TAKEAWAYS

If you've made it this far, you've just about sealed the deal. Understanding how to do this is a fine art, and you better be ready to put on your negotiating shoes, because in commercial property there's plenty on the table to negotiate.

To get the best deal, you need to do your homework thoroughly. Be sure you know what you're getting yourself – and your money – into, and that you're not entering the negotiations with any emotional baggage. The good thing about commercial property is that it's all about numbers, so it's a lot easier to be logical and clinical around decision making.

Next, learn to be a good listener. Don't give away anything without insisting on something in return. And always negotiate in good faith. If you're a serious investor, chances are you'll do business again with the same agent. Treat them with respect, and they'll return it in kind in the future.

STEP 7
MANAGING THE PROPERTY AND UNDERSTANDING THE TAX

This last step is very exciting. It marks an important milestone in your property journey. You have made your property purchase. You've done the hard yards, and now it's time to watch the rent roll in.

But before that happens, you need to work through the options for managing the property. Basically, you can either manage the property yourself or pass the job on to a property manager, for a fee.

As we've outlined, each option has pros and cons. The big positive is that you will learn on the job. You will be able to see for yourself exactly what is involved when it comes to property management, and this knowledge will be very useful when you next invest. Now you've learned how the system works, you'll be able to make a much more informed decision on whether or not to engage a property manager.

Going solo can be stressful, time-consuming and expensive. Of course, this is something you can only learn through experience, but from our side of the fence, engaging a property manager is the only way to go. Full stop.

However, if you do decide to save some money and try doing it yourself, a few fundamental elements you'll need to account for are:

- tenant selection
- advertising
- vacancy risk

- repair costs
- day-to-day management
- tenancy gaps.

Still sound appealing? A good rule of thumb is that the better the lease, the easier the property management. It's also important to set up the ownership structure correctly, so that you can reap the benefits of reducing your tax obligations.

Managing a commercial property

There are a few different ways to manage a commercial property. While the ideal setup for your situation is best left to the professionals to decide, it's useful to understand what your options are, because the best structures offer significant tax benefits.

Professional management

Here are the main advantages and disadvantages of engaging a professional property manager:

Pros:

- They save you time.
- They organise everything for you.
- It helps you at tax time (monthly statements are great for tax returns).
- They deal with the tenants directly.
- They help minimise vacancy.

Cons:

- Their services cost you approximately 4 to 6 per cent of your rent.
- Managers can change, leaving you exposed.

To summarise, your property managers will deal directly with your tenants on all matters. This can be very useful if you are a busy professional, or even if you're retired and travelling the world. Knowing a manager is responsible for your tenants and your property can be a burden lifted. Also, a manager can find you new tenants faster than you could yourself, because they will usually have a large database of other rentals from which they can seek tenants. However, their fees are significant. (Note that in some cases you can pass on the cost of rental management as an outgoing to your tenant.)

It's also worth noting that many people prefer to self-manage, which leads us to the next section.

Self-management

Here are the main advantages and disadvantages of managing your own investment property:

Pros:

- It saves money (no management fees payable).
- Some people like being closely involved with their investment property.
- You may put more care into your property than a rental manager.

Cons:

- You don't receive monthly statements.
- You need to invest time and effort to manage the property.
- The process is likely to be less organised.
- Some tenants can be difficult to deal with.

No matter which option you choose, you can always reverse your decision. For example, first-time commercial investors often use a rental manager but realise 12 months later that managing their perfect tenant can actually be very simple. So they take over the management themselves.

We managed many of our properties in the early days, but as we purchased more properties the workload mushroomed. We really came to grief when we began to self-manage properties in multiple states. We ran into some vacancies, and having to network with people on the ground to help organise inspections was a nightmare. It ended up costing us more than we saved on management fees. So we won't be doing that again for properties not in our own backyard.

Following are some general guidelines for self-managing:

- Ideally you will have some experience with managing people.
- It's much easier if you live locally to your investment property.
- You need to be willing to be involved in the day-to-day activities of your property.
- You will need to deal directly with the council, tenants, maintenance contracts and so on.

If any of this doesn't sound like you, use a professional manager.

Managing and understanding your tax obligations as an investor

Generally speaking, commercial investors pay tax on the net rental income they earn from an investment property, plus tax on any profits they make from the sale of that property. However, the government offers commercial property investors numerous discounts, deductions and exemptions to encourage investment. The way that the tax is calculated depends on the type of entity that owns the property.

The great thing about an investment property is that you can claim tax deductions for most expenses incurred while operating the property, including:

- interest paid on a loan used to buy the commercial investment property
- travel costs incurred during visits to the commercial property
- advertising fees
- repair, maintenance and management expenses
- depreciation of the building structure and the assets within it.

While each ownership structure is obliged to pay a different rate of tax, each structure can also claim different types of deductions. In addition to the deductions mentioned above, each ownership structure is often entitled to claim a credit for the GST included in the purchase price, as well as the following discounts and deductions.

Individuals

If you are the legally recognised owner of the commercial property, the rental income is incorporated into your assessable income and taxed at the individual's marginal tax rate.

It's similar for properties with multiple owners. The proportion of rental income attributed to each owner is equal to the size of their legal interest in the property—regardless of any agreements between the owners that state otherwise—and each portion of the rental income is taxed at the rates that apply to each individual owner.

As with residential property, individuals must also pay tax on any capital gains made from the sale of a commercial investment property. The capital gain is added to the individual's assessable income.

Owners will also add goods and services tax (GST) on the sale price if the going concern assumption isn't satisfied. The going concern assumption basically means that both the buyer and the seller are registered for GST, that there is a current lease in place on the property, and that everything necessary is being done to support the continued operation of the business. This means they pay GST on one-eleventh of the sale price and claim GST credits on purchases that relate to selling the property.

But there are exceptions, for example when you use the margin scheme to work out the GST on the sale of a commercial premises or sell the property as part of a GST-free sale of a going concern.

A company

If you own the commercial property through a company, you're liable for 30 per cent tax to be paid on the property's net rental income. This is the same as the current corporate tax rate and is often a lot lower than an individual's marginal tax rate. The highest tax rate sits at 45 per cent alongside a Medicare levy of 2 per cent (for FY2018–19).

Capital gains are also taxed at 30 per cent, unless the company is eligible for one of the four small business capital gains tax concessions offered by the ATO. Like individuals and trusts, companies must also pay GST on one-eleventh of a commercial property's sale price if the going concern assumption isn't satisfied, but they can claim a few GST credits on purchases that relate to selling the property.

A discretionary trust

You can also choose to purchase your commercial property through a discretionary trust. This means the trustee can apportion the rental income from the trust's property to the beneficiaries however they like, on a discretionary basis. The bonus is that you can get smart about tax. You, or the trustee, can apportion the most rental income to the beneficiary with the lowest marginal tax rate. The beauty of this is that only the beneficiaries who receive an income pay tax; the trust itself doesn't pay any tax as it is a flow-through entity. However, the trust must pay GST on one-eleventh of the sale price if the going concern assumption can't be satisfied, but it can claim GST credits.

This is a no go when it comes to negative gearing, though. A discretionary trust can only distribute *income* to beneficiaries, not losses. But capital losses can be carried forward and offset against future capital gains. And beneficiaries that receive capital gains can apply whatever discount their specific ownership structure entitles them to.

Land tax thresholds also need to be considered when using a discretionary trust to purchase properties. Some states, such as NSW, don't allow any land tax threshold for property owned through a discretionary trust. Fixed or land tax unit trusts can be used in this instance to obtain the land tax threshold; however, these types of trusts don't offer discretionary distribution to beneficiaries. Distributions need to be made in line with the unit entitlement.

A self-managed super fund (SMSF)

Another popular way to fund a commercial property investment is through your self-managed superannuation fund (SMSF). It's tricky, time-consuming and expensive, but for the informed investor it offers excellent tax benefits.

This is because rental income funnelled into an SMSF is taxed at just 15 per cent during the accumulation phase, which is a lot lower than most investors' personal tax rate. Better still, it drops to zero once the fund moves into its pension phase.

A couple of things are worth noting. An SMSF pays tax on capital gains, but there are discounts that can be claimed. Furthermore, an SMSF in the pension phase is exempt from capital gains tax.

It is also required to be registered for GST if it owns a commercial property and its annual turnover exceeds $75000. This means that it will need to pay GST on one-eleventh of the sale price if the going concern assumption can't be satisfied, but it can claim GST credits on purchases that relate to selling the property.

An SMSF can also acquire commercial property from a member of the fund or a related party, which is not the case with residential property. The transaction needs to be at arm's length, which means the transfer needs to be made at market value. This is a capital gains tax event for the vendor, but the small business concessions may be applied to help reduce any tax payable.

As for capital gains tax, SMSFs are eligible for a capital gains tax discount of 33 per cent during the accumulation phase, as long as the asset is held by the fund for more than 12 months. This means that the fund pays 15 per cent tax on two-thirds of the capital gain, which is equal to 10 per cent of the total capital gain. And they are eligible for a complete capital gains tax exemption during the pension phase as long as each member's total super balance is under $1 600 000, meaning they don't need to pay tax on capital gains made during this period.

YOUR TAKEAWAYS

Managing your commercial property is a role you can take on yourself or you can choose to engage a professional property manager to do it for you. While a property manager will save you considerable time and effort in the long run, it's also a useful experience to manage one or two properties yourself so you can learn about the pitfalls and mitigate them later as you grow your portfolio.

You'll need to work out the best ownership structure for the property well before you purchase the asset. The costs of unravelling an incorrect structure can be enormous. For example, how does double stamp duty liability sound? Not ideal. It's important to minimise your tax obligations and set up your finances appropriately, depending on your goals.

This should go without saying, but make sure you have a highly qualified property accountant on your team before you purchase a property.

PART II SUMMARY

Having completed our seven steps, let's reflect on our journey so far. Whether you are a seasoned professional or just starting out, there's always something to learn from seeing how others approach the same challenges. And we love it when others use our guidance to help them achieve property success. You now have all the tools you need to buy a commercial property with confidence.

For us, commercial property investment is a measured and informed game of numbers. We've learned the hard way that emotion doesn't help when navigating this world, and neither does trying to do it all ourselves. The stakes are higher in commercial investing, but so are the rewards.

Here are the key takeaways for each of our seven steps:

1. *Money habits.* Don't forget to build strong saving patterns as you save for your first entry-level deposit of $50 000 for a residential property and $100 000 for a commercial property.

2. *Investment mindset.* Developing the right mindset can make the difference between frustration and becoming a higher level of investor. Once you have the right mindset, you can set your goals and confidently work towards realising them.

3. *Asset selection.* Understanding how the market moves will give you a better foundation on which to make informed decisions. Read up, listen and learn whatever you can.

4. *Method of sale.* Learn to adapt to each sales method according to the property you're interested in, so you won't be let down because you're unfamiliar with a particular sales technique.

5. *Finance.* Your bank is about to become your best friend. Without it, you're hamstrung, so it's worth making sure that you understand thoroughly how to finance your property.

6. *The negotiations.* We have learned through practice that good negotiation is not just about putting your hand up. It takes careful management, timing, and of course not letting emotion get in the way.

7. *Managing the property and understanding the tax.* Understanding the key to the right ownership structure can make a huge difference to your portfolio. It's always worth investing in professional advice.

It takes years of investing experience to truly understand what makes the market tick, but a solid grasp of what happens when, and how best to respond to it, provides a fantastic learning tool.

How do you really accelerate in the commercial property market? What do you need to know that goes above and beyond what you read about in the newspapers? In the next part, we've done the heavy lifting in order to reveal our Top 5 Property Plays. These are the strategies you can use to get ahead of the game and start building your wealth. As you'll expect by now, they'll take you far outside your own backyard.

OUR TOP 5 PROPERTY PLAYS

If you've made it this far, you're already miles ahead of the game. Because most people don't understand how the property market really works, and they're especially uncertain about taking that next step from residential to commercial property.

The seven steps we worked through in the previous chapters are the template we use every day, with every deal, so it's safe to say you now possess some real world, informed knowledge and information. You have also neatly sidestepped those who claim to be experts, like Uncle Bob talking about why you shouldn't invest in commercial property but instead concentrate on buying that house down the road. Which as we all know could be a big opportunity cost for your financial future.

So what's next? You need to know when to climb down off the fence and when to sit it out. But if you can't recognise a good deal, how will you know when to act?

The enduring topic of Australian property always makes headlines. Wouldn't it be nice to be the one telling the story? But to be the storyteller, you must stick to one strategy and become *extremely* good at it.

When it comes to strategies, everyone has their own play. Whether it's a renovations, developments, high yielding assets or just a long-term capital growth strategy, some deals will yield better results for your personal situation. Picking the correct path is critical for you to reach your financial goals. You need to be informed enough to make sure you're the one who gets to pull the right trigger. And the way you do that is by learning what works and what doesn't.

Normally this would come down to experience—trial and error when working to get a deal over the line. But we've been there, and after being involved in over $1 billion in real estate purchases, we've learned a lot about the best property plays. Of course, this didn't just happen. Our insights have accumulated over many years. They helped us to become extremely astute in our investment decisions and secure great deals because we know precisely what we're doing. This book is about 'buying your time back' through building substantial passive incomes with property. For us, the fastest and most efficient way to do this was though high-yielding commercial real-estate.

We continue to fine tune our approach to make sure we're investing only in the properties that suit our longer term goals, and while this will inevitably change, we know what we want, where we want it and how much we are prepared to pay for it.

In this final section of the book we share with you our Top 5 Property Plays to show you how best to use commercial property to your advantage.

Following are our Top 5 Property Plays:

1. *How to build a $100 000 passive income.* Without a doubt, this is the most common question we are asked. How do you do it?

2. *How a property can pay itself off in 10 years.* Sounds great, doesn't it? We'll take you through the numbers so you can see for yourself how this strategy works.

3. *Adding value through a commercial property lease.* We'll show you how to identify a value-add opportunity and how to execute it.

4. *Check the numbers or you may overpay.* This is a good one. It's easy to get seduced by the agent's sweet talk. But never forget they're not working for you.

5. *Syndication: what's in it for you?* You've heard of syndicates, but how do they work and why should you sign up for one?

Let's get started!

HOW TO BUILD A $100 000 PASSIVE INCOME

Of all the property questions we're asked, this is by far the most popular. Middle-income earners are understandably fascinated by the prospect of retiring early from the workforce, and a $100 000 per annum passive income is a common objective. It seems to be the magic number for many, whether they are seeking early retirement or the flexibility to work or not as they choose.

For early investors this goal may seem all but unattainable, but we can tell you it's not. At the time of writing, 11 years after we purchased our first property, we have built a portfolio that produces almost $500 000 in passive income. Proof, if needed, that time, effort and persistence pay off.

Creating a passive income should be one of the main goals for any property investor, because without an income from your investments you'll find it very difficult to pay for your retirement. Which is why we chose this strategy as our top property play.

So what does it take?

Hopefully by now you've gained valuable insights into what it requires to build up a portfolio like ours. But there are of course thousands of variations on how to attract $100 000 passive income through commercial property. For example, you might purchase multiple smaller properties or one larger asset, take on more or less debt, or draw on a residential property to loan into a commercial asset.

What interests us is creating a $100 000 passive income using *as little cash as possible*. Table 16 (overleaf) offers a simple demonstration.

Table 16: cash flow returns based on different debt levels and interest rates (commercial)

Price	$2 000 000	(net of outgoings)
Rent	$160 000	
Depreciation		
Rental mgt	5 per cent	

	Purchase price ($)	Annual rent ($)	Depre-ciation benefit ($)	Interest ($)	Rent mgt ($)	Cash return ($)
Cash buy	2 000 000	160 000	0	0	8000	152 000
70 loan @ 3.5%	2 000 000	160 000	0	49 000	8000	103 000
75 loan @ 3.5%	2 000 000	160 000	0	52 500	8000	99 500
80 loan @ 3.5%	2 000 000	160 000	0	56 000	8000	96 000
100 loan @ 3.5%	2 000 000	160 000		70 000	8000	82 000
70 loan at 4%	2 000 000	160 000	0	56 000	8000	96 000
75 loan at 4%	2 000 000	160 000	0	60 000	8000	92 000
80 loan at 4%	2 000 000	160 000	0	64 000	8000	88 000
100 loan @ 4%	2 000 000	160 000	0	80 000	8000	72 000
70 loan @ 4.5%	2 000 000	160 000	0	63 000	8000	89 000
75 loan @ 4.5%	2 000 000	160 000	0	67 500	8000	84 500
80 loan @ 4.5%	2 000 000	160 000	0	72 000	8000	80 000
100 loan @ 4.5%	2 000 000	160 000	0	90 000	8000	62 000
70 loan @ 5%	2 000 000	160 000	0	70 000	8000	82 000
75 loan @ 5%	2 000 000	160 000	0	75 000	8000	77 000
80 loan @ 5%	2 000 000	160 000	0	80 000	8000	72 000
100 loan @ 5%	2 000 000	160 000	0	100 000	8000	52 000

Net yield: 8 per cent

As you can see, different debt levels and interest rates will affect the final net income. At the time of writing, some commercial interest rates were as low as 2.59 per cent, so this table is actually conservative in the current market.

In this example, the purchase is a $2 million commercial property, with a net yield of 8.0 per cent. We focus here on the 70 per cent debt level at a 3.5 per cent interest only amount. After 100 per cent of the outgoings were taken out (plus an extra $8000 for rental management and 70 per cent mortgage costs), the commercial asset will return a passive income of $103 000 per annum. Sounds good, right?

Let's look a little deeper and put those numbers in perspective. Say you owned three residential properties worth $700 000 each and they were all completely paid off. You would have $2.1 million worth of property assets. Good stuff, yeah?

However, at a gross yield of just 4 per cent, your gross income on your debt-free property would be only $84 000. Then you'd need to subtract the costs of rates, water, maintenance, rental management and insurance from this rent, which would be at least $14 000, leaving only about $60 000 per annum. You would also need to factor in income tax payable on your $60 000 rental income.

Considering you now have a portfolio worth $2.1 million with no debt, a gross pre-tax income of $60 000 is not exactly the return you'd be hoping for. Yet this is what most investors achieve when they invest in residential property.

Table 17 (overleaf) makes this crystal clear for you.

To sum up, the three houses with a total value of $2.1 million require an eye-watering $2.1 million plus in purchase costs of equity/cash to produce a net annual income of $58 120. Our commercial example, on the other hand, requires the use of only $600 000 plus purchase costs to produce an annual income of $103 000.

We'll leave you with that thought … You can see why we prefer commercial property.

And here's another thought: the numbers always tell the true story. But you already knew that, right?

Table 17: commercial vs residential cash flow returns

Property	Current value ($)	Total loan ($)	Total LVR (%)	Annual rent ($)	Interest ($)	Rent mgt ($)	Repairs (assumed) ($)	Insurance, water, land rates etc. ($)	Total costs ($)	Pre-tax cash return ($)
3 houses at 4% gross yield (no debt)	2100000	0	0	84000	0	5880	6000	14000	25880	58120
Commercial property (with 70% loan)	2000000	1400000	70	160000	49000	8000	0	0	57000	103000

YOUR NEXT MOVES

- Develop a savings plan to purchase a commercial property. Allow for at least $100 000 as a deposit plus costs to invest in an entry-level commercial asset. The savings plan goal matched with your $100 000 income goal (or whatever your income goal is) will form the basis of your future investment decisions.

- Structure your purchases correctly. For this you need a highly skilled accountant who is experienced in commercial property structures. It's important to know the differences between purchasing in your own name, through a trust and using a company structure.

- Work with a highly experienced commercial mortgage broker. Many residential specialist brokers do not have the same access to good commercial loans as the experienced ones do. For example, I have seen some brokers obtain 80 per cent commercial loans from the same bank from which other mortgage brokers could secure only 70 per cent. It's also important to have a broker who can find you loans with favourable (and long) terms. This will help with your future serviceability.

- When investing in commercial property, make sure you have buffers in place and purchase quality assets that can be relet. There's no point chasing high commercial yields if you are purchasing risky assets that create reletting stress if your tenant vacates.

- Always compare apples with apples. As you can see above, have a look at the income your deposit can generate for you. In our example, $600 000 in commercial can generate nearly double the income as $2.1 million cash in residential. Again, the numbers tell the true story!

HOW A PROPERTY CAN PAY ITSELF OFF IN 10 YEARS

In a perfect world, we'd have our investment properties lined up in an easy set-and-forget format. We'd sit back and pay them off effortlessly every month until the debt disappears.

Unfortunately, this will remain a pipe dream if you haven't set up your investments the right way. Obstacles have a habit of cropping up when you least expect them, and you'll need to be able to cover them. You could end up having to shell out more than you thought, and this could easily chew into your cash reserves, especially if your goal is to follow us over the fence and pay off your property in 10 years.

What we want to impress on you is that the best way to pay off property is through solid financial planning. And a strong part of this is due diligence. Don't think you can avoid it, because ensuring you have done your homework is your insurance when you seek to pay down debt faster.

Full stop.

While there is more due diligence to do for a commercial property than a residential property, it's worth every cent to get it right. The returns are larger, and you'll also benefit from the capital growth and built-in rental increases.

For this property play, good financial planning involves three key factors: great asset selection, a high yield and a strong continuous lease. This will give you a better chance of uninterrupted cash flow over a long period of time, which in turn will increase the chances of your being able to pay your properties off faster.

In Part II we outlined the best ways to choose your commercial asset. Let's consider two of the most essential aspects of asset selection now.

Higher net yields

Yields must be high enough to produce a positive income from day one—even with 100 per cent debt. Why 100 per cent debt? I like using this rule as many people look to refinance their house to access a deposit for a commercial purchase. Since you are increasing the debt on your home, you need to work from 100 per cent debt calculations, so you have all of the interest rate costs covered in your cash flow equation.* You may remember that earlier in the book we talked about hitting a yield ceiling in the residential market, which is what prompted us to hop over the fence into commercial.

Back then interest rates were higher for commercial loans, so properties on the market at the time had higher yields than they do today. The yields may never return to those glory days, but it's worth keeping in mind that everything is relative. Right now, interest rates are so low that the cash flow can be even better than it used to be, even with lower yielding commercial properties.

In 2020 we are still finding quality, tenanted commercial properties in capital cities with yields of between 6.5 per cent and 8 per cent—extremely good yields considering most of our clients are getting commercial loans with interest rates around 3 per cent. This difference in the interest rates versus yields on offer is currently allowing us to enjoy some of the highest cash flow we will ever see in a property market (at any period). It's why we see so much value in commercial investments right now.

---

*The 100 per cent debt is from borrowing the deposit from your home. For example: you have a $1 million home with $500 000 debt. You might increase your loan on your home to 80 per cent. This means your new home debt is $800 000. However, because the debt is higher you have access to a cash loan amount of $300 000. You can use this as a deposit on a commercial property. This $300 000 can be used to buy a $1 million property once a new loan is written. So your $300 000 is a loan and the $700 000 amount to buy the $1 million property is also a loan. Hence, 100 per cent debt.

Strong debt reduction strategy

Once you've selected your asset with a good yield in place, your next aim is to reduce the debt faster. A great method of achieving this is to use the high net incomes from your commercial properties' rent to pay down the loans over time. This will allow you as the commercial property owner to pay your debts down to zero in half the time of a standard 30-year loan contract—sometimes even sooner.

A high-yielding commercial property can pay itself off in 10 to 13 years. The high cash flow from the net lease can be so strong that if you can put the surplus rent back into your mortgage or offset account, the debt will rapidly reduce without your having to make any extra payments.

If you have a strong lease in place, you'll also benefit from the built-in annual rent rises, which will help you pay off the property even faster each year. Interest rates come into play too, and these typically start at 3 per cent for a commercial property depending on the lender and whether you opt for fixed or variable.

Using the handy debt reduction calculator on our website (www .rethinkinvesting.com.au/property-investment/calculator/), as illustrated in figure 1 (overleaf), you can plug in the numbers on a commercial property to discover how long it would take to pay off your debt.

In this example the property has a 7 per cent net yield and 3 per cent annual increases in its rent. The property is completely paid off in 11 years, without the owner having to inject any of their own funds.

More importantly, this property offers a passive income of $80 169 with zero debt at year 11. Table 18 (overleaf), also drawn from the RI calculator, shows the numbers for the first 10 years. Note: If this particular property had 4 per cent increases or a 7.5 per cent initial net return, the debt would have been squared off in under 10 years. Some of the properties we have found our clients have had yields over 9 per cent but, as previously mentioned, there is a balance between yield and risk that should be carefully maintained. For example, there is no point having a property with a 10 per cent net yield if its re-leasing qualities are poor, as this will lead to longer vacancies should your current tenant ever leave, and longer vacancy periods would obviously lengthen your loan payback timeframe.

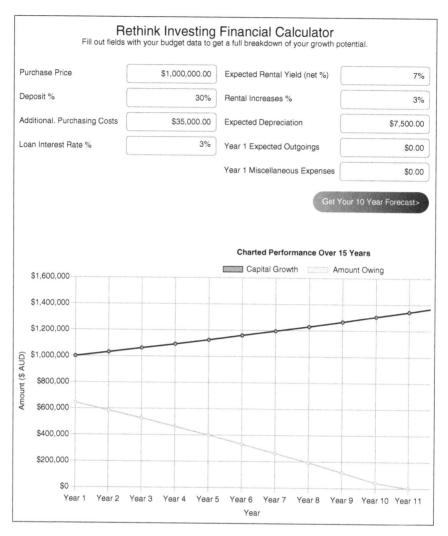

Figure 1: Rethink Investing debt reduction calculator

These types of returns can only be gained from commercial property, which is why this is an extremely important asset class for investors looking to speed up their journey towards early retirement.

The table doesn't factor in vacancy or tax; however, many properties can have the same tenant for decades. There are also good tax benefits for commercial property through depreciation. So, depending on the tax structure you're using, there may not be a large amount of tax payable, which will keep your costs down.

Table 18: investment performance over 10-year period

Expenses	Year 1	Year 2	Year 3	Year 4	Year 5	Year 6	Year 7	Year 8	Year 9	Year 10
Loan interest	$21000	$21000	$21000	$21000	$21000	$21000	$21000	$21000	$21000	$21000
Outgoings	$-	$-	$-	$-	$-	$-	$-	$-	$-	$-
Miscellaneous	$-	$-	$-	$-	$-	$-	$-	$-	$-	$-
Annual expenses	$21000	$21000	$21000	$21000	$21000	$21000	$21000	$21000	$21000	$21000
Rent										
Rent with 3% increases	$70000	$72100	$74263	$76491	$78786	$81149	$83584	$86091	$88674	$91334
Depreciation	$7500	$7500	$7500	$7500	$7500	$7500	$7500	$7500	$7500	$7500
Total cash income pa	$56500	$58600	$60763	$62991	$65286	$67649	$70084	$72591	$75174	$77834
Capital growth (cap rate 7%)	$1000000	$1030000	$1060900	$1092727	$1125509	$1159274	$1194052	$1229874	$1266770	$1304773
Amount owing on loan	$643500	$584900	$524137	$461146	$395860	$328211	$258128	$185536	$110363	$32582

Each step may require more work than when purchasing a residential property, and you do need a higher deposit, but with the right financial set-up you'll be able to pay it off faster—the numbers speak for themselves!

And once it's paid off, you'll be able to enjoy the solid passive income generated by the rental payments. That's where the real 'lifestyle' benefits kick in!

YOUR NEXT MOVES

- The key to an effective pay-down strategy working well is to have continuous rent coming in. Focus on properties with long-term tenants who appear to be staying for a very long time. For example, a vet or dentist, or a warehouse leased by an established business happy in their location. Properties that are under-rented also indicate there's less chance the tenant would want to move elsewhere for a better deal.

- Aim for properties with strong relettability, so if you ever did lose your tenant, you could replace them quickly.

- Work hard to make sure you have the best financing deal. An interest rate 1 per cent lower on average could reduce your payback period by an entire year. For more information, check out the payback calculator on our website: www.rethinkinvesting.com.au/property-investment/calculator/

- Pick properties with high yields. It goes without saying that the higher the yield, the faster you can reduce your debt. Just be careful not to chase a deal solely on the basis of its high yield, as this might lead to a riskier purchase.

ADDING VALUE THROUGH A COMMERCIAL PROPERTY LEASE

This property play is about drilling deeper into the lease and the type of asset that will deliver you a value-add opportunity. Over the years, we've developed our own preferences and recommendations, and we are excited to share them with you. Because not all commercial properties are created equal, you'll find that going about it the right way, including taking account of our recommendations, could mean the difference between your getting an okay return and an outstanding one.

The property

But first things first. Before you start bidding on properties you must determine what type of commercial property you want. It's almost as important as choosing between shares and houses, as each subsector of the commercial property market can perform very differently depending on the economy.

We've introduced you to the key asset types and our recommendations for where to invest based on factors such as location, visibility, parking and layout. But we want you to get more bang for your buck, so let's drill deeper into which properties can deliver the best results.

As you know, there are many different property types and, depending on the economy and other factors, they will perform differently at different times. Following are examples of commercial properties we like (and some less so). The case studies illustrate clearly why these particular properties are high performers.

Industrial

Right now, we are having great success in finding our clients quality on and off-market industrial properties in price points as cheap as $300 000, to more than $10 million. But no matter what the price, when they are well-located industrial properties that have good access to local amenities, tenants can be easy to find. The best types of tenants include trade-related businesses, mechanics, next-day delivery companies, online businesses, manufacturers, cool-room storage or any other type of storage businesses, and engineering companies. COVID-19 hasn't been a big disruptor for many of the types of businesses that operate out of industrial warehouses. We have also found a lot of retail businesses sped up their move to the online world throughout this period. This has meant more demand on storage as more businesses need to store their product for online sales. We all know the Amazon story, right?

CASE STUDY
Industrial site attracts 8.1 per cent net return

We secured this investment for one of our clients late last year. It's a freestanding industrial property located 40 minutes from the CBD of a capital city. It has a large site area of 3180m² and a net lettable area (NLA) of 1100m². The property comes with an existing long-established tenancy (more than nine years) in place, with a three-year lease and a three-year option. After all the outgoings have been taken out (including interest costs on a 70 per cent debt) our buyer is left with a $71 010 passive income. A great outcome!

We like properties like this because it has a large land component, is a strong non-discretionary spending type of business and offers room to raise rents to the market value, which increases the asset's value. More on that topic in a moment.

Negotiated price: $1 362 500

Current rent: $101 294 per annum

Current yield: 8.1 per cent net

Retail shopfronts

Retail properties are often the easiest types of properties to understand if you have a residential investor background, because most people can relate them to their own retail consumer experiences. As a result, this can make retail investment a popular category, which in turn can cause yields to be lower than they typically should be for their specific quality compared to other asset classes such as office and industrial properties.

Location is absolutely crucial to the performance of many retail properties, which tend to charge higher rent per square metre than other commercial property types. For these investments, good foot traffic for their specific customers is essential, and they need to have the right balance between neighbouring tenants too. For example, you wouldn't want too many hairdressers competing for business in one location.

CASE STUDY

Shopping centre purchased for $11.8 million attracts 8.22 per cent net return

We acquired this high-yielding, fully tenanted shopping centre on behalf of our client for $11 800 000. The property has an excellent tenancy mix of 12 tenants (80 per cent medical/health and supermarket). The centre is performing well even under COVID-19, as there is a high proportion of medical and supermarket trade keeps the centre strong.

This was a good investment because it had a high car space ratio mixed with a lot of essential service–type tenants that will perform well in any economic condition.

To be clear, we're not big fans of many types of retail investments. As mentioned, there is a general weakness in the retail shopfront markets. However, there are well-tenanted exceptions well worth pursuing – for example, multi-tenant investments like this one, allied medical-type tenants in retail precincts, or any retail property that has a solid trading history and you're confident there is a need for their services into the long term. Look for 'destination' retail assets – such as hairdressers, dentists, and cafes – where you need to visit the physical store to use their services so it cant be moved online.

Negotiated price: $11 800 000

Current rent: $971 500 net per annum + GST

Current yield: 8.22 per cent net

Office space

Many different industries need an office from which to operate, which ensures a wide pool of potential tenants. Often office tenants are high-quality tenants too, as professional firms are more likely to maintain the building and fit-out to a higher standard than other commercial tenants.

Car spaces are extremely valuable in office properties. A higher car space to floor space ratio can make your property more attractive to tenants and as an investment.

CASE STUDY

Office space with a secure government tenant

We acquired this high-yielding asset with a five-year lease to an National Disability Insurance Scheme-backed tenant for a client for $420 000. After all the outgoings were taken out (including the interest costs on a 70 per cent debt), our buyer was left with a $22 450 passive income.

This was a great investment because securing a five-year government lease at a yield this high pretty much guaranteed the client exceptional returns for this period. There's no reason to believe they wouldn't stay for at least another five years either.

As we've noted, the office market has a lot of weakness right now caused by the COVID-19 disruptions to the workplace. However, we have found that many suburban office spaces like this one have done well through COVID. Many businesses still need office space and local offices with good car park ratios in smaller complexes have proved to remain in high demand.

Negotiated price: $420 000

Current rent: $35 280 net per annum + GST

Current yield: 8.4 per cent net

Speciality

Outside the three main types of commercial asset classes is the speciality sector. This is for single use properties such as carwashes, child care centres, service stations, and so on. There is added risk in this sector as if the tenant financially fails for your property site, it could be more difficult to find a new one. However, as the businesses themselves are often worth money, the owners simply won't let the them fail if they are wanting to retire or move on. The business itself is instead sold on to a new operator and part of the businesses value is associated with a strong lease. So speciality commercial properties are known to have strong leases.

CASE STUDY

Veterinary centre purchased for $1 125 000
8.35 per cent net yield

This deal, secured for our clients in mid-2020, was purchased totally off-market and only Rethink Investing got to see it. We were pretty excited to lock this one in as it was a was rare opportunity to purchase a one-of-a-kind veterinarian property with a 8.35 per cent net yield. There was a strong 7+6 year lease where the tenant pays 100 per cent of the outgoings, including management fees and land tax. The property comes with freehold 950m² of land.

This investment will produce the new owner a passive income of $1,384 per week even after the mortgage and 100 per cent of the outgoings have been accounted for. For some, this could lead to instant retirement. Think about this number deeply before you rush off and buy a residential property.

Negotiated price: $1 125 000

Current rent: $93 940 net per annum + GST

Current yield: 8.22 per cent net

The research

Once you have found the type of investment you like it's time to drill down into that asset class to find a great deal. And part of making a deal great could be a value-add opportunity. (Note that we have mentioned only four types of commercial property in this section, but the same principles can apply to, for example, medical properties.)

One of the easiest methods of adding capital value to your commercial property is by increasing the rent, as values of commercial properties are largely driven by rental returns or the potential for capital growth.

To determine if there is an opportunity to add capital value through rental increases, you need to understand what the going square metre rate is for similar properties in the area. If the tenant is paying $180/m^2 and every other similar property in the area is renting for at least $210 m^2, there is a potential to raise the rent by $30 m^2. This would represent a 16.67 per cent increase in the rental value. If you purchased it at the old rental income, then your value of the asset could also increase by 16.67 per cent.

Now let's be honest, you can't just crash your way in there and hit the tenants for an extra $30/m^2 from day one. It will take time and negotiating skill to raise the rents to the fair market value.

The first step is to negotiate the rental rate when you can legally do so. For example, if the lease has three years left to run, there isn't much you can do. However, if you are within 12 months of lease expiration, there may be an opportunity to negotiate with the tenant early on, especially if they love the property and want to stay.

We find that sometimes tenants don't understand the current state of play in the market, so showing them a spreadsheet with all the other square metre rates in the area can be a good way of enlightening them and helping you to justify a rental increase. This is a great strategy to use when the tenant is paying below market rates. It also takes some of the emotion out of the negotiations.

You can easily research comparable properties for lease online (using sites such as CoreLogic) to see how the property you're interested in stacks up.

It's worth keeping in mind that most property leases are based on cost per square metre plus outgoings, with GST usually payable on top of rent. So make sure you look at the total costs of the outgoings in your rates.

If it all gets too confusing, a good local rental manager will be able to take over the lease negotiations for you.

Rent review

Another way to slowly build capital in a commercial property is simply to allow the rent to increase over time. If you are negotiating the lease yourself, this could be an opportunity to add value at a faster rate. As we've discussed, most leases have an annual scheduled increase built into them. We outlined in Part II how, as the rent grows, so does your commercial property's value.

There are a few options for annual rent reviews. You can set them to coincide with the CPI (Consumer Price Index), which is the most common approach. A fixed percentage increase is the other main option, with 3 per cent the most common increase; 4 per cent is considered a big increase and anything above that is recognised as very high. Most tenants would find a 4+ per cent increase unsustainable for their cost base.

It's worth remembering that different markets have different rules, but most use the CPI or 3 per cent.

What this means for your return on investment is that with each annual price increase you'll see more cash coming in each month. Also, when you revalue the property, the higher the rent the more equity you may be able to release.

The lease terms

Another way to add value is to increase the security level on your property. The longer the lease, the greater the security. This was the first value-add we personally made. As mentioned earlier, we were able to increase the lease on our supermarket from 12 months to five years. This increased the valuation as soon as the lease was confirmed.

Incentives

When it comes to locking in a good lease, you have a card up your sleeve — a lease incentive. This is a common practice between office landlords and tenants. You've probably seen examples on the drive to your local shops: '$10 000 fit-out incentive! Two months' free rent!' and the like.

Incentives can take several forms, such as rent abatement, a rent-free period or a fit-out contribution, but basically they're a sweetener to attract tenants.

If you're looking for tenants in a market with high vacancy rates, you'll need to offer whatever inducements you can — with careful consultation with your team — to lock in a tenant.

You can also use incentives that fluctuate depending on the market. You can adjust the incentive a little if there's less competition, or more if the vacancy occurs during a period of high demand.

Finally, incentives are used to offset fit-out costs. It's common for tenants to be able to afford the rent but not the fit-out, so adding in a fit-out incentive can help secure a great tenant. The better the quality of tenant, the more your commercial property will be worth in the long run. So it's important to remember that incentives are an important part of securing high-quality tenants.

Types of tenants

As we learned in Part II, finding the right tenant can make or break a high-performing investment, for as well as knowing where to look for them, understanding the types of tenants that are better than others will deliver more bang for your buck.

Here are our tips on the best types of tenants.

Medical properties

Medical tenants are brilliant. They're often very stable as they are backed by non-discretionary spending type customers. By this I mean that customers need to visit these properties regardless of the economy, which makes them very attractive tenants for investors. Often zoning for medical tenants is more restrictive than for general retail even though they can be in similar locations.

The negatives are that the yields are often lower because people pay more for medical versus other types of tenants. And if you lose a medical tenant it can be harder to find another, as the pool is smaller than for other types, which can create longer vacancy periods. Prices for medical properties can be as low as $300 000 for a small office suite all the way up to tens of millions of dollars for large, freestanding, purpose-built medical centres.

Government tenants

These tenants are found mostly in office or retail formats. Government tenants can make for an incredibly stable investment because they don't rely on turning a profit. Government-funded tenants rely on grants from taxpayers, and leases are generally at least three years, with six-year leases also common.

Prices start from about $400 000 but can reach into the millions depending on the floor space required for that government tenant. Some examples of a government tenant may include electoral offices of local MPs, NDIS offices, EPA offices, health, education and transport departments.

Restaurants and cafés

These types of properties are very common and can be a great investment when the location and business operator are right. Leases are typically three to five years and properties tend to have an owner-operator as tenant. These types of tenants generally can't move location easily, so if they're running a good business, they could stay with you for decades.

The risk is buying into a property where some less established operators run their margins thin. By this I mean that any drop in trade could place the tenant in financial stress.

Things to consider for this type of tenant include local competitors, the experience of the operating tenant, the quality of the kitchen fit-out, foot traffic and online business reviews. Prices can be as cheap as $200 000 for a small, hole-in-the-wall café, to many millions for a prime, fine dining restaurant on Sydney Harbour.

Professional service tenants

These tenants are solicitors, accountants, engineers, financial planners, IT consultants and the like. I love these types of tenants as they run businesses that are often viewed as 'essential services'. They're located in offices that can be in the CBD or in local suburban boutique office blocks.

Stability is what first comes to mind when I think of this category of tenant. Prices generally range from $300 000 for a small regional office to about $2 million for a larger office. We love them.

Dentists

Dentists are another essential service–type tenant. The difference between a dentist and other types of allied medical ones is their fit-out. The cost of setting up a dentist can be upwards of $500 000, which means it's very costly for a dentist to pack up and move. Generally, they make a good living, so they'll often remain at the same location for decades.

Prices for a dentist can be as low as $500 000 for a small regional practice up to about $1.5 million for an average-sized metro practice. It's worth remembering that these tenants often come with lower yields. However, they're very stable, so investors are generally happy to accept a lower yield.

Real estate offices

These types of businesses make money from sales commissions and rent rolls. They pick prominent retail/office locations where there is a signage opportunity, which is the main reason why you see many real estate agent offices in corner block locations with big glass windows displaying not only the properties they are selling or renting, but also their brand. Prices generally range from $750 000 to $1.5 million. The leases vary widely, offering plenty of flexibility.

Bottle shops

Bottle shops can be resilient in both good and bad economic times, especially in a country like Australia, where people love a drink. Typically, bottle shops will be part of a strong national company that holds the lease over the property.

Leases are usually at least five years. Bottle shops can be as cheap as $500 000 for small regional shopfronts all the way up to around $5 million for a metro shop with drive-through facilities.

Hotels and resorts

This isn't the best place to get started, but many experienced investors find it a fun and profitable area. Of course, other investors have lost their shirts working in this category, so make sure you know what you're doing.

Land development

Land development is one of the most exciting types of commercial real estate. However, it can also teach you some quick and painful lessons if you jump in too fast.

You need to be very detailed in your budget and feasibility study. There's no point buying the land if you can't afford to build what needs to be built. The tough part is once it's built, you need to find tenants. So, it can be a long time before you start collecting an income on your investment.

These are just a few examples of different types of commercial properties and their associated tenants. But before you do anything, you must learn about the market and how different types of businesses are performing. You need to put in the time to understand where the opportunities are in the economy. For example, COVID-19 has caused weakness in the CBD office market but brought strength to industrial assets. There is no real shortcut in property plays, unless it is in hiring professional help from a buyer's agent.

We have found that far too often people go into commercial property with little understanding of the diverse range of asset types available. If you are not specific in your search and well prepared, you are likely to find much in the process confusing. Below are some of our top tips on how to bridge the knowledge gap.

YOUR NEXT MOVES

- Find out where the leasing markets are strongest by reading property reports from major valuation and real estate agencies.

- Once you have decided on your preferred subsector, work with agents, leasing managers and/or a buyer's agent to locate prospective properties in the field you have chosen.

- Always invest in properties that can be easily relet. If you are not confident you can replace the tenant within a few months, then maybe the rental market underpinning your property's value isn't strong enough.

PLAY 4
CHECK THE NUMBERS OR YOU MAY OVERPAY

Before you're ready to give up residential for commercial, you need to be sufficiently educated to identify the risks. But this is tricky when there's so much misinformation about commercial property ready to trap the novice investor. Like any type of investing, the risks are there, but it's about identifying them and managing them to better your chances of making a profit.

So for this property play we are going to focus on ensuring you don't pay any more than you need to. After all, you want your money in your pocket, rather than in someone else's, and having strong literacy around commercial investing will give you the knowledge you need so you know exactly what your money will get you.

Let's talk about that sense of excitement you feel when you come across what looks like a really good deal. Your heart beats a little faster and you skim over the details to get to the most important bits. When you have limited experience investing in a new asset class, it's hard to know what you're in for, but suddenly you're in competition with many others who may be more experienced and are ready to beat you to the deal. We've frequently been in the position where we have to submit an offer by a deadline, with no time to spare, even when waiting on due diligence information.

So you need to think on your feet to manage your risk, complete your due diligence and get the deal done. Luckily, there's a process you can follow to ensure you tie up any loose ends. Get it right and you'll be on a much surer footing when it comes to the deal.

Offer subject to due diligence

Welcome to 'offer subject to due diligence'. We touched on this in Part II, but basically it is a purchasing option that can buy you some time to get to the bottom of your property's due diligence.

It's worth mentioning that this won't always work because due diligence allowances are not always accepted, but they can be very valuable.

CASE STUDY
Due diligence check

In this example, one of our clients nearly paid too much for a property based on incorrect numbers supplied by the agent. We'll show you how it played out and how we saved our client a lot of money.

In 2019 we helped the client purchase a multi-income commercial property. It was advertised as producing a $134 005 gross income with outgoings of $17 490 per annum. This indicated a net income of $116 515.

Remember, net income is what you work off to calculate value as an investor. If the net income is higher, the property is worth more. If the net income is lower, the property is obviously worth less.

The agents were asking $1.6 million, which represented a net yield of 7.5 per cent. After some solid negotiating, our buyer's agent managed to secure the property for $1 425 000, which represented a net yield of 8.18 per cent.

A contract with a 21-day due diligence clause was drawn up for our client. This meant the contract was conditional on us completing our due diligence.

So far, so good.

But as we carried out our due diligence, we noticed that there was approximately $5000 worth of outgoings that the agents had missed in their information memorandum. Now, that price difference might not sound enormous, but when you back calculate it against the yield you can see it had a major impact on price:

Net rent (expected): $116515   **Net yield (expected):** 8.18 per cent

Net rent (actual): $111515   **Net yield (actual):** 7.83 per cent

By submitting an offer subject to due diligence, we were able to triple check the outgoings of the property and confirm that our buyer was worse off from a net income perspective.

Our next step was to renegotiate the price down prior to going unconditional on the contract. From our point of view, the fairest result was to lower the price to secure the original 8.18 per cent net yield.

So we went back to the agents and asked for a $50 000 discount prior to going unconditional on the contract. This didn't get us to the exact 8.18 per cent but it got us within reach of it, at 8.11 per cent.

Net yield (after $50 000 discount): 8.11 per cent

After a lot of hard back-and-forth negotiating with the agent/owner, the owner accepted the discount request and the property settled a month later.

As you can see, even a $5000 variation in outgoings had a major impact on the price. So always remember to check the outgoings!

Furthermore, the agents often present approximate numbers as outgoings, so if you don't check them you may end up with a property that is not generating the assumed income, which can mean overpaying for the property when it's too late to renegotiate the lease.

Agents represent the seller, so they will generally underestimate the numbers to help the vendor get a better price. Also, remember that while agents do their best to present the exact correct information, it's in their best interest to do so, sometimes they are supplied incorrect information from the vendors themselves. It's up to you to cross-check everything.

Buy a property with excellent relettability qualities

Buying properties that can be relet without difficulty is a cornerstone of good investing. It's so important because if you lose a tenant, you can market the property and find one sooner rather than later.

Remember the old story about commercial properties having longer vacancies? Well it's true, but if you buy the right property in the right area you should not have much trouble finding a tenant. This will cut down the costs of lost income but also keep your current tenants in the location longer.

One key to getting this play right is knowing the leasing market very well. Unfortunately, there are no real shortcuts for investors, and you will need to do the work on the ground by speaking with the relevant leasing professionals, who can help paint you a true picture of what the rental market is like.

These days we're very lucky because we know the market extremely well. We live and breathe the commercial property market and we're constantly helping clients to purchase properties. At the time of writing, we have been helping our clients purchase 3-5 commercial properties per week across the country.

It's likely you won't have this depth of experience, but that's okay. What you need to do is find similar properties you can compare to the one you're trying to buy.

One trick we use is to jump onto the CoreLogic property website. If, for example, we're looking at a 500m^2 warehouse, we'll view similar-sized vacant properties and see how long they've been on the market. You'll be able to source the data on the average vacancy period of similar warehouses and qualify it to, say, a three to four months' vacancy, which is a workable period you can allow for. Following is a general definition of the vacancy periods we use:

- 1–2 months. Very tight market with minimal leasing risk
- 3–4 months. More balanced market with minimal leasing risk
- 5–6 months. Slightly weaker market with moderate leasing risk
- +7–12 months. Weaker market with higher leasing risk
- 13–24 months. Extremely weak market with an unacceptable leasing risk.

In general, if you find it's taking more than six months on average to find tenants, this should probably be a market you avoid. The market is telling its own story, and you're likely barking up the wrong tree.

YOUR NEXT MOVES

- Use online property search tools such as CoreLogic to view vacancy periods.

- Speak with as many rental managers as you can to determine how they feel about the market on the ground. Please note: some people will have a vested interest in talking you into or out of a deal, especially if you are buying a property from a competitor.

- Be ready to put in the time. If you are trying to understand the leasing market, you will need time to build up your knowledge on the ground. A great way to fast-track this is to visit areas in person.

- Don't be afraid to pay for a buyer's agent. They know the market from an investor's point of view better than most.

SYNDICATION: WHAT'S IN IT FOR YOU?

Syndication's a buzzword in commercial property circles right now. And for good reason.

Basically, syndication allows you to acquire a portion of a high-value commercial asset. It guarantees you a split of the rental income and enables you to 'shoot higher' than your budget would otherwise allow. Sounds good, right?

So what is a syndicate?

A syndicate is an organised group of individuals, corporations or entities. It can also be professionally run as a managed fund. The group works together to pursue and promote their collective business interests.

Here's another way of looking at it that most people will be familiar with. In a lottery or horse ownership syndicate, a group of people pitch in to buy a ticket or own a share of a horse in the hope they'll win big. If they do, the winnings are divided between the individuals who form the syndicate.

A commercial property syndicate works along similar lines. But rather than relying on the long odds of these examples, a commercial property syndication *guarantees* a split of the rental income and capital growth profits of the asset or assets the syndicate controls.

The benefits

There are some fantastic benefits to forming syndicates in the commercial world. Let's start with the best ones.

Purchase 'out of reach' investments

A group of independent investors in a syndicate can pool their money to create a deposit on a high-value commercial investment they could not afford on their own. The size and scale of these assets, high-quality tenant covenants and solid, long-term rental returns on offer simply wouldn't be accessible to most individual property investors on their own.

For example, you would have the reach to buy retail centres, industrial facilities or office buildings. Through a syndicate, you can bid for these assets and have a much greater chance of sealing the deal.

Free leverage

Many, if not most, syndicates have what's called a 'non-recourse' bank loan within the syndicate structure. This means that if the borrower defaults, the bank can seize only the assets put up as collateral for the loan. The lender can't seek further compensation from the borrower even if the assets used as collateral don't cover the full amount of the loan.

For example, the syndicates we have been involved in normally have an LVR of around 50 to 55 per cent. This means that in a $10 million syndicate, $5 million of that total amount of funds will come from a bank loan, with the other $5 million as cash from the syndicate members. This means your money is leveraged without your having to go visit the bank yourself.

Then the $5 million in cash can be split up into 'units'. So, if you invested $500 000 into the syndicate with a 50 per cent LVR, you would essentially control $1 million worth of property because the bank doesn't own units in the syndicate. The $500 000 would mean you own $500 000 out of the $5 million—or 10 per cent of the units in the syndicate. And that means you're entitled to 10 per cent of the cash flow and capital growth profits. This can be particularly useful when you don't have the ability to get a loan yourself. For this reason we use the term 'free leverage' — because it's a loan you probably couldn't have otherwise secured.

Save time

Most syndicates are set up by professionals who manage the purchasing process and the running of the investment fund. You generally take a back seat when investing in a syndicate. That means less time spent having to manage your investment yourself. However, only a well-managed property syndicate unburdens you of your time and energy. If you are the one running the syndicate, it can be a full-time job, so watch out!

Less money down

In many cases, you can invest in a syndicate with lower amounts of capital. As we've described, to purchase a property on your own you need at least $100 000 for the deposit on an entry-level commercial property. However, managed syndicates backed by an Australian Financial Services Licence (AFSL), may allow you to invest with much less. This could be as low as $25 000, but every syndicate has its own rules on minimum deposit levels.

What's the catch?

Like most benefits in life, syndicates have drawbacks too. We'll explain these in some detail so you can better evaluate if a 'direct' or a 'syndicate' purchase best suits your situation.

Less control

Perhaps the greatest drawback of syndication relates to working with a group. The longer you need to hold the investment with others, the greater the chances that your goals will diverge from those of other syndicate members. For example, at the start of the property acquisition you might all agree to hold the investment for seven years before selling. However, during the seven-year period some members may wish to exit the syndicate sooner than planned. This could cause problems for relationships within

Rethink Property Investing

the syndicate, but given the long-term nature of investing in this asset class, any relationship issues must be managed.

Less leverage

Generally, investors in property syndicates prefer not to provide personal guarantees. Banks will typically provide non-recourse loans if the LVR is 55 per cent or less. So a 55 per cent debt is normally the maximum you'll be able to achieve. This is less than the LVR — up to 80 per cent — if you purchase commercial property on your own.

More fees

There are several fees associated with investing in a syndicate managed by a fund manager. There can be a 1 to 3 per cent fee on the acquisition purchase, a 0.5 to 1.2 per cent annual management fee and a 1 to 2 per cent sale fee when the asset is sold. Obviously, these fees diminish the return. Equally obviously, when you invest directly you won't have to pay ongoing fees other than your interest costs and taxes.

Setting up a syndicate

So how does it work and how do you set one up? Here's what you need to do:

- Find property partners who share the same goals.
- Work with a highly experienced accountant and solicitor to set up the correct structure (for example, a unit trust).
- Use your unit trust to make an offer on the property. Make sure you allow yourself enough time to raise the capital and secure the bank loan.
- Work with a skilled mortgage broker who can source the best loan for your syndicate.
- Agree to distribute the funds back to the investors each month or quarter.
- Draw up an agreement on how long you will hold the asset.

CASE STUDY
Two properties in one syndicate

The best way to illustrate this property play in action is through sharing our own personal experience. A couple of years ago, we teamed up with a client to participate in a syndicate purchase of two assets. We liked the idea of just using cash and not having to go through a lending process to purchase a direct investment. It was also a way of diversifying our portfolio, as we had recently purchased several commercial properties. A syndicate seemed like a sensible next step.

Besides ourselves, the syndicate comprised six others, and the deal involved purchasing two multi-tenant commercial properties. (Just so you know, WALE is an acronym for weighted average lease expiry. It is basically a measurement of the general time frame when all leases in a property will expire. It's good to know because it indicates when the property is likely to fall vacant.)

Property 1

- Multi-tenanted shopping centre with extra land for future STCA development. Set on a 5823m² block of land in south-east Queensland.

- Three of the well-established tenants are household names – IGA, The Bottle-O and Chemist Warehouse. The WALE was 5.2 years.

- Original sale price was $4 400 000. We negotiated $395 000 off for the syndicate.

- The current rent is 15 per cent below current market rates, giving the investor added opportunity to boost the net yield. The net yield was 7.7 per cent.

- The site offers opportunities for future development, with the possibility of adding a car wash STCA.

Property 2

- Multi-tenanted shopping centre on prominent corner block of 3025m², providing a net lettable area of 1387m².

- Fully leased mixed-use commercial asset.

- Fully leased to 10 separate tenants.

- Property consists of three separate buildings.

- 8.7 per cent net return.

- Strong WALE.

Structure of the fund

- The two properties were worth a total of $10 500 000.

- They had a total net income of $873 000.

- Their total net yield was 8.31 per cent.

- A 65 per cent loan was used to secure the property. That meant the other 35 per cent plus costs were cash provided by the syndicate (the eight investors).

- The result for us, and for the other investors, was we had put in our own cash to create cash returns of around 11 per cent, plus capital growth. We didn't have to speak with a bank, yet we got to enjoy these leveraged returns in high quality assets.

The result

We were able to join six like-minded individuals who had a common goal – to maximise their passive income. These two high-yielding investments did exactly that. The risk was spread between many different tenants, which gave us more security over the income.

To syndicate or not?

It's worth noting that the leveraged return for a direct investment can be just as good, if not better, than a syndicate due to the higher loan rations. Table 19 (overleaf) illustrates this by showing the difference between investing $200 000 through a syndicate versus through a direct purchase. Assuming growth and yield are identical, you will make a greater return on equity for one reason alone: direct investments allow for higher leverage.

To summarise, the returns in syndicates are often lower compared to investing directly, when you get it right. Investing directly as an individual essentially means higher leverage, more control and less fees. But the risk can be higher because you are dealing with the asset yourself without the protections that may come with a well-managed syndicate. It's worth having a chat with a qualified commercial buyer's agent, who can help you remove the risk and improve your chances of a higher return.

Table 19: comparing a syndicate to direct investment

	Syndicate	Direct investment
Net yield	7 per cent	7 per cent
LVR	50 per cent	70 per cent
Deposit invested	$200 000.00	$200 000.00
Controlled property amount	$400 000.00	$666 666.67
Assumed capital growth (4% pa)	$16 000.00	$26 666.67
Total return cash flow	$22 000.00	$32 666.67
Total return on equity	19%	30%

YOUR NEXT MOVES

- Make sure the property suits your individual needs. For example, if you are comfortable with investing in medical or industrial properties, this should be your target for a syndicate purchase. Essentially, you need to treat a syndicate purchase with the same level of oversight and interest as if you're purchasing the property direct yourself.

- You still need to do your due diligence, as you would with any deal, and not just assume that because others are investing you don't need to worry about it.

- Understand the overall plan of the syndicate and make sure it aligns with your own investment goals. For example, many syndicates have five- to seven-year hold periods. If this is too quick for you, then maybe it's not the syndicate you should buy into.

- Understand the fees involved. There's normally an acquisition and disposal fee for the property, and an annual managed fee for many AFSL-operated syndicates.

- Before joining a syndicate, be sure to compare the returns proposed to those if you purchased a commercial property on your own. In our experience, direct investing can often trump syndicate returns.

PART III SUMMARY

What we love about our property plays is that we haven't simply pulled them from a book or read about them somewhere. They work because we've done them all ourselves. We stepped off the fence and jumped into a new backyard because we recognised a good deal when we saw one. Our hope is that you are now better equipped to grasp this too.

Here are our key takeaways for each of our Top 5 Property Plays:

1. *How to build a $100 000 passive income.* Develop a savings plan, structure your purchases and work with a commercial mortgage broker.

2. *How a property can pay itself off in 10 years.* Buy properties with higher net yields, and lock in a strong debt reduction strategy.

3. *Adding value through a commercial property lease.* How to identify a value-add opportunity and how to execute it. Understanding the market and the lease will deliver great results, but it's also about specific property and tenant types.

4. *Check the numbers or you may overpay.* Do your due diligence checks to ensure everything lines up and buy properties that can be easily relet.

5. *Syndication: what's in it for you?* Buying out-of-reach properties can accelerate your profit, but you need to ensure the property suits your needs.

CONCLUSION

Congratulations, you've made it! How do you feel now that you've finished the book? Excited? Overwhelmed? Tired? You've invested the time and energy to get to the end, and we appreciate it's been a lot to get your head around. As with any new learning, you may feel many different emotions by the time you reach these last few pages.

We've introduced you to the ways we think work best, as learned over many years. We've shared some of our highs and lows on the journey towards winning our financial freedom through commercial property investing. Wherever you are on your property journey, we hope you'll be able to draw on this book to learn something new about jumping over the fence into the land of commercial.

We'd like to leave you with a few thoughts to keep in mind.

Why invest now?

For decades, residential property investment has been the number one option for mums and dads seeking a comfortable and secure retirement. If you have owned one or more investment homes, you're already familiar with residential processes and how to juggle the various moving parts when buying and selling your properties.

Our whole philosophy is that the residential market is not the be-all and end-all of investing in real estate. For most property investors, commercial property is still not 'relatable'—in fact, it's downright unsexy. Most of us wouldn't swoon at the notion of owning an industrial-size shed on a concrete floor, as we might over a heritage home with a salt-water swimming pool. Or stand around the barbecue chatting about the local office market or how industrial tenants are evolving. Commercial property is generally far less familiar and understood, so there's a huge knowledge gap. This is exacerbated by a general lack of dialogue, less media coverage and less conversation about commercial property in everyday life, which limits opportunities for broader education. It should be said, though, that we're beginning to see indications that commercial investing is becoming more popular.

The fact that on any given day commercial tends to be more profitable than residential is never lost on us, because it's confirmed by almost every transaction we make for our clients. Sure, commercial may still be unfamiliar, but we have found it to be an excellent way to start or to expand your portfolio.

In fact, as we noted in the introduction, now is one of the best times in history to invest in commercial real estate in Australia. Not only does Australia enjoy record low interest rates, but also the cash flow benefit has never been stronger for commercial investments compared to residential. This is because they are by nature more binding, with longer lease periods. Also, commercial properties have a higher yield than the residential market as their capital growth rate is lower.

What's happening in the market right now?

As this new decade unfolds, we are seeing a trend towards yield compression. This means investors are paying more for a commercial property relative to the rental income. This will make finding commercial gold trickier, but it also means there is good capital growth on offer now, and as the year unfolds and the yields continue to tighten, the focus will be on getting the jump on properties sooner than other players.

There are four main reasons for the market's current yield compression:

- *Lower interest rates.* At the time of writing, interest rates were at record lows. This has made finance cheaper, which justifies more spending on commercial real estate as the cash flow returns are so attractive.

- *Shortage of stock.* This has become a persistent obstacle for many commercial sales agents around the country. Without much stock to sell, it's harder to earn a good living. The main cause for this shortage of stock is the lower interest rates. When rates are low, fewer investors are selling. Their commercial assets are growing in value but are also providing them with good incomes. Many tenants are also looking to purchase commercial property to occupy, so tenanted investments become scarcer and in greater demand.

- *More residential investors are seeking cash flow assets.* Many investors are defaulting to commercial property following volatility in the share market in recent times. For example, the COVID-19 global stock market crash, which began on February 20, 2020, has had a huge impact on global economies. The rest of the year has been exciting on the commercial property front. Strong growth is reported, as it was for the previous five years. Specifically, there have been some big improvements in industrial markets, where many markets have achieved double-digit capital growth. Conversely, office markets have been the weakest, while retail has had mixed results.

- *The search for yield has never been stronger.* In 2020 and beyond, one of the biggest challenges for all types of investors is achieving high yields in their various portfolios. Share payout dividends (passive income for shares) are less certain and residential yields are already at record low levels. This means more investors are seeking cash-flow assets in the commercial space to generate higher returns. The stability of price is one of the redeeming factors attracting investors to all types of Australian real estate and this extra demand will put upwards pressure on values (capital growth!).

Who's performing best in 2021?

It's worth mentioning that not all commercial properties are created equal. For example, industrial properties have been performing increasingly well in recent times while large sectors of retail are struggling in certain areas, with almost weekly reports of big retailers moving into administration. Some of these assets are already reeling from poor trading profits through a combination of the growth of online sales, plus the recent influx of competition from some major overseas traders.

Industrial properties are benefiting from the retail shift because many online companies need warehouses to store their goods for online sales, which creates great opportunities for commercial investors. As the industrial sector is principally focused on logistics, distribution, manufacturing and storage, there is a general flow-on effect for industrial storage space as physical shopfront retail activity slows. At the same time, these retailers are reducing their retail shopfronts because they are generally not as efficient as online marketing, dollar for dollar. There is also increasing demand from office property operators in our capital cities as our economy is shifting towards service-based industries. The takeaway is that the commercial real estate market in Australia has gone from strength to strength in recent times.

We expect growth to be more even across the country rather than restricted to Sydney and Melbourne, the high-growth areas over the past five years. What this means for you is that you'll have a much greater opportunity to invest in commercial property.

E-commerce

We believe the rise of e-commerce commercial investments will continue to represent excellent opportunities in 2020 and beyond. E-commerce is having a positive effect on the industrial market as an investment asset, and we've seen more interest in this space from investors overseas and at home.

This has been driven largely by retailers requiring more space, as well as the increase in growth across the online retail trade sector. According to

June 2019 figures from the ABS, Australia has seen a year-on-year growth rate of about 20 per cent in the online retail trade sector.

As a result, we expect to see more players entering the e-commerce market, while existing investors will continue to seek out even better deals. All of this adds up to a tightening of available space and greater demand for industrial floorspace.

Office

Office vacancies continue to fall, which means that opportunities for leasing remain strong. This is leading to office demand not only in established markets like Sydney and Melbourne, but also in capital cities like Perth, which is usually a high-vacancy city.

There will be an economic recovery following the COVID-induced recession. In 2020 there was a massive government stimulus, which took many forms. Other things we expect:

- Interest rates will dip even further.
- Yields on office property will tighten.
- The industrial sector can expect strong capital inflows.
- Office market rents will grow at an even pace.
- Capital growth will pick back up in 2021.
- Investment activity will increase due to lower interest rates.
- Demand for commercial property will increase.
- Demand for owner-occupiers will increase.

Are you up for the challenge?

No doubt about it, commercial property remains a road less travelled.

While many of our clients say commercial property is the 'end game' for their investment goals, rather than the starting point, many other investors don't even get that far. Going against the flow can be daunting. They'd rather throw commercial property into the too-hard basket and hunker down safely in their own backyard.

You know now that the numbers tell a very different story, as we have illustrated throughout this book. We have shared many stories and case studies showing how in fact the numbers tend to stack up better for commercial property than for residential property.

Our goal has been to demystify commercial investing, because when you understand how it works, and better appreciate the risks and rewards, you'll be more likely to consider commercial property earlier in your investment journey—perhaps even for your very first investment.

You'll need to stay positive on your journey. There will be hurdles, and trends will come and go, so it's up to you to have the right mindset to tackle problems and adjust to changes as they crop up.

Keep moving forward

Two final pieces of advice: never let a single issue bring you down, and never forget what you're aiming for.

As we write this, Australia is in the midst of the COVID-19 pandemic. No-one can predict with any certainty what's on the cards for any market, let alone the commercial property market. Commercial property investment has no one-size-fits-all solutions. Like any market, it will continue to fluctuate with changes in the economy, supply and demand, and regional and global events.

Reverses can either undermine you or provide you with valuable object lessons. Don't expect property investing to be easy. It is a lifelong journey, throwing up ever-changing challenges. Whether it's a global financial crisis, news of the departure of a longstanding tenant or a large unanticipated maintenance bill, it can all be very disheartening or even overwhelming.

It's worth remembering that when things go pear-shaped there's always a solution. You're steering the ship, so sit back, work through the steps, and make sure you have a clear understanding of where you are headed and how your portfolio will get you there.

When issues arise, go back to basics. Do your research and your due diligence; get your mind clear and you'll be in a better place to make the right decisions. By remembering that asset classes change every couple of years, depending on the economic situation, you can make it a little easier to ride each wave.

Life always moves forward—and so will your investing portfolio. We like to think that as it grows and develops, so will you alongside it. If you don't have the stomach for it, you won't be able to handle the load. With the right mindset, you'll make sure that the small bumps along the way stay small, and actually help yield life-changing financial benefits for you, your family and your future.

The annual review

We advise our clients to sit down once a year and refocus their plans and strategies. It's important to review your goals and revisit what you want to get out of investing.

This is easier if you're a couple. Being a team of two can be a big advantage, because when your goals are aligned you can create more momentum and sustain it over a longer period.

Don't be afraid of sitting down once a year—or even every month or week—to discuss your financial goals. Remember that working towards a retirement income goal is what sets professional players apart from part-time investors.

Remember too that it's okay to ask for help if you don't have all the answers or knowledge. Whether you seek advice from experts in specific areas, or you just need a good broker or commercial buyer's agent on your books, there's plenty to gain from recruiting professional help.

We've seen too many people fall into the trap of wanting to do it all themselves. Knowledge is power, so don't hesitate to seek out opportunities to learn from others who have more experience than you. It's so important to surround yourself with the right team—people whose judgement you can trust because they've done it all before.

The last word

Mina

For me, the best part of this journey is adapting to our ever-changing goals. Whenever the goalposts shift, I draw out something new that I've learned, because I believe in always moving forward with new learnings. But I make sure to keep my eye on the prize too. Which is spending more time with family and being able to travel as much as I want, whenever I want, winning back time to live life to the fullest and enjoy every moment.

When I look back over our investing journey so far, I feel I'm exactly where I should be. The best part is enjoying good cash flow as well as good capital growth on the properties we have bought over the years—it feels as though we've got the best of both worlds. We played our cards right and did the right groundwork whenever we went into a property deal.

I believe one of our biggest mistakes was putting our money in a principal place of residence at the start of our investing career. That's because no investment driven by emotion will ever give you back money or passive income. As we've said, you don't want to fall into the emotion trap, because buying on emotion is not a good way to invest and can complicate things immensely.

However, we did it and we learned from the experience. And we used it as leverage to buy our next principal place of residence. We sold it because the cash flow was poor, which was hurting our lending capacity. So it wasn't all bad.

Today we're much more calculating. We look at our outgoings and mortgage repayments. We have a standard of only investing in a yield of 6.5 per cent and above. However, this yield can be compressed for various reasons such as getting a property with a large amount of land or buying into a very tight market. As interest rates drop, 6 per cent is looking like our new minimum. We focus on commercial properties with long leases.

Scott

While we always like to look forward, it's also helpful to go back and learn from our mistakes.

My biggest regret was that I didn't get into commercial property earlier. You might think that retiring at 28 is young, but the truth is we didn't seal the deal on a commercial property until we had over a dozen residential properties. Some were not the best performers in terms of cash flow *and* growth. Had I jumped over the fence half a decade earlier, we would have saved ourselves a lot of hassles from dealing with large numbers of residential tenants we are still managing today. Commercial property was just so much more streamlined and efficient for us, which is why I wish I had known even earlier what I know now.

But find me a successful investor who's never made a mistake, and I'll be shocked! You'll be hard pressed to find anyone alive who hasn't put a foot wrong.

The problem with mistakes isn't in making them, but in giving up as soon as you do. It's perfectly normal to stuff up deals along the way. What distinguishes good investors is that they learn through their daily practice and continuously finetune their processes over the years.

Personally, I've learned more from my mistakes than from my successes. They've made me a better investor. I believe all investors should be more open about what's worked for them and what hasn't.

One of my biggest fails was a few years ago when we bought a site in Adelaide. I thought it was a prime site for development, which is not something I'm experienced in and is not part of our regular strategy. But given my appetite for risk, I thought, why not? I was looking for quick gains, and here was my perfect opportunity.

We bought it at a low point in the market, and we overpaid for it, which resulted in a bad yield. The market was too quiet, and I didn't do my research properly. My problem was that I got emotionally fixated on the idea of doing a development, which was a commercial property 101 error! Of course it blew up in my face. Not spectacularly, but enough to become a mistake on our journey. Sometimes you just need to take the loss. If something bad happens, you can fix it, and you shouldn't look to offload it straightaway in a knee-jerk reaction.

The big lesson is that investment is a long game. You need to think of commercial property investments as requiring many years or even decades sitting in your portfolio, because that's when the benefits will truly be experienced.

Today we are incredibly proud of where we are and what we have achieved. And we have only really just begun our journey. We have plans to acquire another $10 million in commercial property in the next 5 years alone. We know that the hard lessons and tough decisions, and our commitment to not accepting the status quo, have got us where we are today, with the kind of passive income we only dreamed of way back when we were sitting on that beach in Greece.

For those of you who are ready to join us, there's no time like the present to look over the fence and rethink your investing journey. We couldn't be happier to share our knowledge so you can benefit from our experience. When you're ready, we'll be happy to welcome you into our backyard!

If you're looking for help investing in the lucrative world of commercial property, please visit www.rethinkinvesting.com.au

ACKNOWLEDGEMENTS

It takes a lot of people to write a book, and we were certainly not alone in this journey.

First and foremost, we would like to thank our family, specifically our parents Nada and Chris (Mina's parents) and Lyn and Laurie (Scott's parents) and our extended families. Thank you for being there and supporting through this journey. And to the newest member of our family, Willow, thank you for being the brightest star in our universe, everything we do is for you.

To the Rethink Investing team, we couldn't ask for a better work family. Your dedication to our cause, to help everyone achieve their wealth goals, is what helps us get up in the morning. Thank you for your help and patience while we were writing, and for always supporting us when things get difficult.

We would like to thank Elle Radin at Studio Panapo, for your expert creative guidance over the years and support with this book. To Annie Reid from Atrium Media (www.atrium.media) for her patience, guidance and overall support throughout the writing of the manuscript. To the team at Wiley, Lucy, Chris, Ingrid, Francesca, Bron, and Renee, thank you for believing in our idea, and helping us every step of the way to edit, publish, and market the book.

To our clients, thank you for believing in us, for seeing the value in commercial property investing, and for trusting us with your investment strategy.

Finally, thank you to you, the reader, for considering us as your guide to the next phase in your investment journey. These steps and plays have worked well for us, and we're certain they will work just as well for you.

COMMON COMMERCIAL REAL ESTATE TERMINOLOGY

If you are looking to buy, lease or sell commercial or industrial property then you're going to have to liaise with many industry professionals such as agents, accountants, lenders, solicitors and property managers.

Below are the definitions of some of the common commercial real estate terms that you're likely to come across. The more you learn, the easier it will be for you to cut through the overwhelming commercial jargon!

Amenities: The features and benefits of a property that create value. Tangible amenities could include onsite parking, while intangible amenities might be the proximity to local transport or retail outlets.

Anchor tenant: The is the main tenant in a leased commercial property who generally attracts other tenants and/or people to the property.

Appraisal: An informal estimate of the price of a property, usually provided by a real estate agent. An appraisal is not the same as a formal valuation.

Annual Percentage Rate (APR): The annual rate charged for borrowing, or made as a result of investing, expressed as a single percentage value. This represents the actual yearly cost of funds, or income from investing, over the term of a loan.

Arrears: Overdue payments on a debt or liability. When one or more payments have been missed on an account that requires regular recurring payments, such as a mortgage, rental agreement, utility bill or any type of loan.

Asset Management: Activities or services designed to maintain and increase the market value of any asset so the owner can benefit from returns. In real estate, asset management focuses on maximising property value and ongoing returns from the property, usually in the form of rental income.

Asking Rent: The amount of rent a landlord is advertising for a space. Quoted as the dollars per square foot, per year.

Building Code of Australia (BCA): Written regulations created and maintained by the Australian Building Codes Board, setting the minimum standards of health, safety, amenity and sustainability for the construction industry. The BCA details technical requirements for the design and construction of buildings in Australia.

Capital: In general, this refers to financial resources available for use. Capital can be used to generate wealth when it is invested or used to produce goods and services. It can also be combined with labour to produce a return. Capital in the form of property can be rented out to generate income.

Conveyancing: The process of transferring property between a buyer and a seller. In real estate, conveyancing involves drawing up and carrying out a written contract that sets out the agreed purchase price and the date of transfer, as well as the obligations and responsibilities of both parties.

Contingencies: These are items that need to be met, changed, or remedied in order for a deal to close.

Contiguous space: Two commercial spaces that are adjacent to each other, either on the same floor of a building, or that sit directly above or below one another.

Counter offer: A new offer made by a seller or buyer on a property in response to an unacceptable offer by either party.

Covenant: A condition in a real property deed or title that limits or prevents someone from using a property for certain purposes.

Consumer Price Index (CPI): The average change over time in how much households pay for a fixed basket of goods and services. In Australia, the Australian Bureau of Statistics publishes CPI figures. The CPI can indicate changes in economic inflation and variations in the cost of living.

Depreciation: The reduction in value of a tangible asset over time. With real estate, depreciation can also mean a drop in the value of property assets due to poor market conditions.

Due diligence: Investigating a potential investment or purchase to confirm all material facts. When someone is preparing to purchase a property, the buyer needs to examine, among other things, the contract of sale, and the planning controls in place that will affect how the land and/ or buildings are used.

Effective rent: The actual amount of rent paid on average per year.

Fit-out: Preparing a leased space for occupation by a tenant. This may include the installation of things such as floor coverings, partitions and signage. Fit-outs are usually a tenant's expense, but this can sometimes be negotiated.

Fixtures: Fixed parts of a commercial property included in a sale, such as light fittings and carpet, as opposed to loose items like furniture, which are often excluded.

Gross area: The total floor area of a building, usually measured from its outside walls.

Gross Lease: Tenant pays base rent and increases in operating expenses over an expense stop or base year.

Gross Leasable Area (GLA): The floor area that can be used by tenants. Generally measured from the center of the joint partitions to outside wall surfaces.

Heads of Agreement (HOA): The agreement with a prospective tenant before the lease is signed.

Land Tax: An annual tax on the value of a piece of land. In Australia, land tax is administered by the state and territory governments.

Lease: A document that outlines the terms and conditions for a tenant to occupy a commercial property for a set period.

Leasehold: That there is a lease in place with the freeholder, also known as the landlord, to use a property for a number of years.

Lessee: The tenant of a leased commercial property.

Lessor: The owner of a leased commercial property.

Minimum divisible: The smallest area allowed in the division of a property.

Mortgage insurance: An insurance policy that the lender or borrower can purchase to protect themselves against mortgage default. In Australia, Lenders Mortgage Insurance (LMI) is usually required for mortgages greater than 80 per cent of the property value. In most cases, the borrower pays the insurance premium for LMI.

National Australian Built Environment Rating System (NABERS): A national rating system that measures the environmental performance of buildings in Australia. NABERS analyses 12 months of performance data relating to a building or tenancy's energy or water bills, or conducts a waste audit, and provides a star rating. This rating is scaled relative to the performance of other similar buildings in the same location.

Negative gearing: Borrowing money to buy an asset and receiving income, other than funds used to cover the loan interest and maintenance costs, from the investment. In Australia, the shortfall between income earned and interest due can be deducted from an individual's tax liability. Negative gearing becomes profitable when the property is sold, assuming that property values are rising and a capital gain can be made. Investors considering negative gearing must have the finances to fund their ongoing interest and maintenance costs until the property is sold.

Net Leasable Area (NLA): In a building or project, floor space that may be rented to tenants. The area upon which rental payments are based. This generally excludes common areas and space devoted to the heating, cooling and other equipment of a building.

Real Estate Investment Trust (REIT): An investment vehicle for real estate, whereby investors can buy a stake in property assets, including buildings and mortgages, without tying up their capital in the long term. REITs can be traded, like stocks, on major exchanges. They give investors exposure to large-scale real estate assets, including warehouses, hospitals, shopping malls and apartment buildings.

Sale and leaseback: When a company sells their building to an investor and then signs a long-term lease for the space, providing income for the investor.

Stamp duty: A tax on legal documents that relate to the transfer of assets or property. Property sales and acquisitions throughout Australia are subject to stamp duty, although rates vary in each state and territory.

Strata title: A form of ownership created for multi-level apartment blocks, and horizontal subdivisions with shared areas such as car parks and swimming pools. Strata title properties consist of individual lots and common property.

Sublease: A lease or rental agreement between a tenant who already holds a lease to a commercial space or property and another party, called the sublessee or subtenant, who wants to use part or all of that space.

Tenants in common: The co-owners of an undivided interest in the same property. Each has an equal right to the possession and use of the property. Each owner can bequeath their interest to beneficiaries through their will. In contrast, in a joint tenancy, if one party dies their share passes automatically to the remaining owner or owners.

Term deposit: A deposit held at a financial institution for a fixed term that may range anywhere from a month to a few years. The conditions of a term deposit are that the money can only be withdrawn after the term has ended or by the borrower giving an agreed number of days' notice.

Typically, a longer term will offer a higher interest rate, and if the cash is withdrawn early, a penalty may be charged.

Torrens Title Property: A property where the owner holds the title to the building and the land it is on. A Torrens Title document will list all details and interests affecting a property and its land, including easements, caveats, mortgages, covenants and past changes in ownership.

Trust account: A bank account set up by one person on behalf of another. For example, an agent may set up an account for an owner to collect a commercial property buyer's deposit.

Valuation: A formal process of establishing the value of a property from an objective and independent point of view. In most Australian states and territories, a formal valuation can only be provided by a qualified valuer who has the necessary qualifications and training.

Yield: The rent that a commercial property currently generates for the owner, expressed as a percentage of the market value of the property.

INDEX

CPSIA information can be obtained
at www.ICGtesting.com
Printed in the USA
FSHW021423250321
79794FS